# Behind the Masks

# Behind the Masks

Gwen Harwood
remembered by her friends

Edited by Robyn Mathison & Robert Cox

All authors' royalties from sales of this book will be donated to cancer research.

*Behind the Masks: Gwen Harwood remembered by her friends*
ISBN 978 1 76041 020 9
Copyright © text individual contributors 2015
Copyright © this collection Robyn Mathison & Robert Cox 2015
Cover photos of Gwen Harwood © Alison Hoddinott
(front, 1995; back, at Halcyon, Kettering, circa 1982)

First published 2015 by
**GINNINDERRA PRESS**
PO Box 3461 Port Adelaide SA 5015
www.ginninderrapress.com.au

# Contents

| | | |
|---|---|---|
| Introduction | Robert Cox | 7 |
| Poet Wondering at the World | Robert Cox | 13 |
| An Unforgettable Educator | Gae Williams | 18 |
| Poet and Paradox | Janet Upcher | 19 |
| The Sweet Singer of Pine Street | Don Kay | 21 |
| First Sight of the Famous Poet | Tim Thorne | 27 |
| A Culinary and Literary Artist | Alison Hoddinott | 29 |
| Madam President | Wal & Berenice Eastman | 34 |
| The Golden Wine of Rest | Stephen Edgar | 36 |
| Demolition Dust and Doulton Cups | Sarah Day | 41 |
| Of Pseudonyms and Serendipity | Robyn Mathison | 43 |
| Dark Deeds and White Lace Collars | Giles Hugo | 50 |
| Observer in the Chaucer Mould | John Chilcott | 53 |
| Mentor, Mother, Mischief-maker | Graeme Hetherington | 56 |
| Contributors | | 80 |

*Gwen in the 1980s. (Photo: Alison Hoddinott)*

# Introduction

## Robert Cox

'I wonder sometimes if the literary pests are writing memoirs: "The last time I saw her she was pale and sick but smiling bravely."' So mused the dying Gwen Harwood in a letter written a few months before she succumbed to cancer. Nearly two decades have passed since she wrote that, but no memoir or biography of the loved and estimable poet has yet appeared. While her poems and the two published volumes of her correspondence enable us to hear her speaking about herself and her life and people and things that mattered to her, in these pages her friends and acquaintances – no 'literary pests', these – tell for the first time of the Gwen Harwood they knew, woman and poet. Their recollections are warm and affectionate and sometimes surprising. Some might even be thought shocking.

Gwen Harwood was extraordinary. She was a major Australian writer with a superb gift for language, which she transmuted into poetry of enduring worth. She did so not in the solitary garret of popular illusion, time-rich and fortified by bottle or bong, but sitting soberly at the family dining table (if it happened to be vacant) in her ordinary suburban home whenever time was left after the domestic demands of husband, children, house and garden had been met. As her fame grew, even that precious time had to be divided and shared with others as she was increasingly called upon to lecture, give readings, appear at festivals, launch books, open exhibitions, serve on literary and parochial committees, play the organ in church, and write critiques of aspiring writers' work, all the while mentoring and even mothering those she thought worthy.

Yet there were even more sides to Gwen than those – enigmatic sides,

sides she disguised with various masks. It is not surprising that Alison Hoddinott, a long-time friend who is a contributor to this collection, included a chapter titled 'Masks and Disguises' in her book about Gwen's poetry. 'I like masks, I like belonging to a carnival,' Gwen told a newspaper in 1978, and the Gwen Harwood who emerges from these collected reminiscences is revealed not only as a woman of mettle and generosity but as a 'true chameleon', in the words of a man who was her friend for more than a quarter of a century. In these pages we are given glimpses of some of the many facets of her character as an assiduous biographer might unearth them – not only of Gwen as a writer but, inter alia, as a musician, a churchgoer, an inspiring educator, a popular FAW official, an adept cook and a keen angler who was often conscience-stricken about killing her catch – and of some of the masks she wore.

There is, of course, a sense in which most creative writers can be said to wear masks. They invent widely disparate characters and create lives for them and even inhabit them, as actors endeavour to do, in order to limn them convincingly. Gwen certainly did. 'I'm a *dramatic poet*; I create character,' she is quoted as saying. But she took the creation of character one step further than most. Early in her career, when editorial indifference to the poetry of the 'Tasmanian housewife' revealed the gender bias then prevalent and inimical to her, she invented several pseudonyms, mainly male, and successfully submitted work under one or another of them, even going so far as to arrange a different return address and create an individual persona for each. Such inventions were persuasive. 'I marvelled at her ability to write with different voices for different pseudonyms, as well as for characters within the poems,' an admiring friend remembers.

Interestingly, as late as 1975, the year her third book, *Selected Poems*, was published and might be thought to have cemented her reputation and obviated any need to wear masks, she was still publishing poems under the pseudonym T.F. Kline, for reasons that appear now to be unfathomable.

Despite all those invented personae eddying around her imagination, Gwen is revealed in these pages as having been blessed with the knowledge of precisely who and what she was and the ability to be wholly that person in any situation. 'Beyond habit, household, children, I am I,' she wrote in her poem 'Iris'. She was a truth-teller in poetry and in person who was never afraid to eschew diplomacy when she had a point to make or a belief to uphold, for she had neither a talent for pretence or fawning nor any need for one. Ask the poetry editor of *The Bulletin* circa 1961.

Alluding to that famous shafting leads inevitably to the subject of Gwen's considerable bent for mischief, one fuelled by a larrikin sense of humour – 'a master hoaxer', one of the contributors to this volume calls her, not altogether with affection. Another remembers her 'ironic response to anything pompous or pretentious', while a third acknowledges her 'barbed wit' but quickly counters any implied negativity with mention of her 'immense kindness'. Similar pairs of adjectival antitheses abound herein and intrigue throughout. She could be 'tough and tender', 'caustic and sweet', 'cynical and accepting', one friend notes, while another perceptively points out that 'These contradictions within her personality are probably what made her poetry so powerful.' Gwen Harwood was truly a complex character, one capable of shocks as well as surprises.

One unexpected revelation is that she had her dark side, or at least an interest in life's dark side. 'If Gwen may be said to have had an obsession,' a long-time friend reflects, 'perhaps it was with the Devil.' Another recalls her fascination with and knowledge of Jack the Ripper, that eternally classic embodiment of the darkness in mankind. Conversely – Gwen the enigma again – a third paints her as a devout churchgoer deeply involved in many aspects of spiritual and parochial life.

All her friends remember her as having had a remarked flair for the preparation and enjoyment of food, especially when it was shared with them or other guests, as it so often was. Corollary to that, she was as generous a guest as she was hospitable a host. 'It was impossible for Gwen to arrive empty-handed when invited somewhere,' a close friend notes. Another remembers that when Gwen visited her home, 'She'd often bring a pot of her home-made jam. At other times she'd bring a book or journal. She'd say, "I don't want this back. Keep it, or pass it on."'

So these recollections reveal a woman endowed with a great ability to live a full, rich life – intellectually, creatively and socially – despite the limitations usually associated with full-time domestic duties, and it is noteworthy that all the poems collected in her first book were written between 1956 and 1961, when her four children were small and/or still dependent. The year that book was finally published, 1963, she re-entered the workforce as a medical receptionist and remained one for a decade while still managing to find time to fulfil her duties to her family as home-maker and to herself as thinker and creative force. Her gift of a prodigious memory, here several times remarked upon, was seemingly honed by the need for her to compose in her head as she went about her diurnal round of domestic and salaried work, the remembered compositions later being committed to paper when chores were finished for the day and space was available at the dining table for her and her typewriter.

Above all, it is as a cherished friend that each contributor remembers her. 'With her, [friendship] was a serious business,' one observes, and her gift for profound and selfless and enduring friendship shines through these remembrances (and was the catalyst for many of her poems), illuminating the woman and the enigma warts and all, with honesty but without slur – strengths and weaknesses, positives and negatives, sweet and sour, yang and yin. Antitheses again. Or perhaps simply a solid mandala, symbol of completeness, of a rounded human being behind the masks.

My own friendship with Gwen was regrettably too brief and sporadic to have become close, beginning, as it did, only about two years before she died. I had admired her poetry since I first discovered it but had never encountered the poet herself. However, one evening in 1993 I heard her launch Claudio Alcorso's book *The Wind You Say* and have a faint memory that her speech was warm, witty and well delivered. After the formalities, as I was standing by myself with a drink in my hand, I saw that Gwen too was standing alone, so I introduced myself and told her of my admiration for her work. We chatted for a while and I was struck by how unaffected she was; despite her celebrity, she was down to earth and modest and friendly. I liked her immediately.

However, it would be an exaggeration to say we were friends thereafter, although we were certainly amiable. But, for one reason or another, all except one of our subsequent encounters were accidental and transient. Yet she always remembered me if we saw each other at a book launch – we both patronised Christopher Pearce's Hobart Bookshop – or on a city street. She remembered my name and always seemed pleased to stop for a few minutes' chat, usually about books or literary gossip.

Unknown to me, during the final few of our chance encounters she was shrouded in the fearful knowledge she was suffering from the cancer that would soon kill her, yet she always appeared cheerful, vivacious and life-embracing. When she discovered that I wrote short stories, she asked to read some, but from timidity or procrastination I never did show her any. I regret that now, certain that her opinions would have been invaluable: perceptive and fearless, although perhaps painfully frank. But I remember well a piece of her practical advice. 'If you're asked to read [in public], you must do so and read well,' she said. 'If you can't read well, go and take lessons. If you still can't read well, get somebody who can to read for you.'

The notable exception to those casual encounters was on 18 August 1993 when I spent the afternoon with her at her home in Pine Street, West Hobart, interviewing her for a profile-style piece about her I wanted to write. I don't now remember anything about the house itself, but I remember with gratitude how generous she was with her time that day, for the word 'interview' does not begin to describe the long afternoon we spent together. No mere short and simple question-and-answer session ensued; instead, we had several hours of sheer enjoyment during which we both laughed a lot, swapped ideas and opinions, and talked about music and books and a great deal else. She also signed my copy of her *Selected Poems* and, with what I now know to be characteristic generosity, made me a gift of a copy of *Freely They Stood Who Stood, and Fell Who Fell*, her 1993 Tasmanian Peace Trust lecture. It was an afternoon to cherish and I do. While the seed of friendship sown at the Alcorso launch surely germinated that day, her diagnosis with terminal cancer only seventeen months later nipped in the bud its full flowering.

The cassette recording I made of our dialogue that joyous afternoon is now lost, but the profile, which I edited so she seemed to be speaking uninterruptedly about herself rather than simply answering questions I put to her, was published soon after in Hobart's *Mercury* newspaper. Later, after Gwen's death, I used some of that afternoon's gleanings to write a different, more objective piece about her for the magazine *40° South*, of which I was then assistant editor. Titled 'Gwen Harwood: Poet Wondering at the World', it appeared in the magazine's autumn 1999 issue. Not having known her well, however, I see now that I might have misunderstood the tone of some of her comments, since posthumous publication of her correspondence has cast doubt on my glib assertion that 'she soon fell in love with Tasmania', and indeed on whether she was ever truly reconciled to living here. Perhaps it is significant that, at her own request, her ashes were scattered in Brisbane, the 'Blessed City' that was her home from birth until the age of twenty-five.

Nevertheless, the piece is reprinted below. It is placed first in this collection solely because it provides a brief biographical overview of the poet and can therefore serve as a useful conduit to the more specific and intimate memories of people who knew her better than I. Her publisher ETT Imprint kindly gave me permission to quote from Gwen's poetry.

# Poet Wondering at the World

## Robert Cox

Pass her on a Hobart street and you probably wouldn't have given her a second glance: a small, slim, sprightly woman with short grey hair cut in a no-nonsense style, plain clothing, a gentle face, spectacles. Somebody's grandmother.

If, however, you were alert and you managed to catch her attention even briefly, it might have given you pause, for her eyes shone with intelligence and perspicacity.

And if you were lucky enough to engage her in conversation, you were quickly left in no doubt at all that here was a woman with a fine mind: the mind of a thinker – a scholar, perhaps, or an accomplished artist. You'd have been right in all instances, for this was the late Gwen Harwood, as intelligent and creative a writer as ever called Tasmania home.

Although the state has been home to several other distinguished poets – Vivian Smith, A.D. Hope, Margaret Scott, Stephen Edgar and James McAuley come to mind – for many readers, none so defined the uniqueness of Tasmania as a place in the world as Gwen Harwood did.

She was incontrovertibly one of Australia's most accomplished and acclaimed poets: a Member of the Order of Australia and recipient of three honorary Doctorates of Letters, as well as the Patrick White Award, the Grace Leven Prize, the Robert Frost Medallion and the Victorian Premier's Literary Award. She won the Meanjin Poetry Prize in consecutive years, 1958 and 1959. Besides publishing nearly 400 poems, she wrote libretti (thirteen in all) for composers Don Kay, Larry Sitsky, Ian Cugley and James Penberthy. She was also a tireless and prolific correspondent, a writer of countless charming, witty, beautifully crafted letters to her many friends. Somehow she also found time to be a wife and the mother of four children and to lecture at schools, colleges, universities and writers' festivals.

Gwen Harwood was born in Brisbane in 1920 and trained to be a music teacher, although, she said, 'I'd always written poetry and always loved writing it.' She came to Tasmania in 1945 as the bride of a naval-officer-turned-university-lecturer and stayed for the rest of her life. Nearly half a century later she vividly remembered the initial shock the island gave her. 'It was another world for me,' she recalled. 'I had not imagined anything like it – the space and loneliness after Brisbane... I remember standing at the old Cambridge airport, looking around at the chill distances, and thinking "This is another world altogether. This is not like anything I have ever seen." It was a feeling of immense desolation, of exile.'

Nevertheless, she soon fell in love with Tasmania and what she came to see as its stunning beauty. Indeed, she credited Tasmania with making her the poet she became. 'In a way, it engendered my life,' she said. 'I'm sure that if I'd stayed in lovely hot old Brisbane, I'd have lounged around doing nothing in particular.'

She further acknowledged that Tasmania had helped her understand English poetry, saying she did not understand it until she came here. 'You read about the seasons, but you have to feel them and see them and get them through your skin before you know what [English poetry's] about.'

The Harwoods settled in a house at Fern Tree, on the slopes of Mount Wellington, a place Gwen remembered thus in a poem:

> Sing, memory, sing those seasons in the freezing
>   suburb of Fern Tree, a rock-shaded place
> with tree ferns, gullies, snowfalls and eye-pleasing
>   prospects from paths along the mountain-face.

Later they moved to the southern Hobart suburb of Taroona, then to Lenah Valley and 'a lovely old house made of Huon pine with lots of rooms and a great garden'. In 1976 she and her husband went to live on a small acreage at Oyster Cove, on the D'Entrecasteaux Channel, the setting for some delightful and moving poems, where they stayed until their 1985 move to Pine Street, West Hobart.

Despite the quality of the poetry she was writing as she settled into life in Tasmania, getting published proved to be difficult. Poem after poem was rejected, and she was riled by the fact that many of the poems published in magazines that had rejected hers seemed inferior to the poems she had had rejected. Then she realised that nearly all the poems being published were written by men, so she began submitting her work under such pseudonyms as Walter Lehmann and had the dubious satisfaction of having it accepted for publication. In a fit of larrikin malice – there was more than a touch of larrikin to her character – she submitted to *The Bulletin* a poem in which the capitalised initial letter of each line acrostically spelt FUCK ALL EDITORS. None of the magazine's editorial staff noticed, and the poem's publication helped to make her famous.

Her poetry reflected her interest in all the world had to offer, from the most mundane aspects of daily life through the beauties of the natural world to music and philosophy, especially Wittgenstein's. Quite antithetical to the obsessive, hard-living and sometimes fey poets of popular myth or misconception, she led a well-ordered life that seems almost perverse in its ordinariness, although her intelligence and her eclectic interests gave her great joy in a great variety of activities. As she said, 'I love the ancient Egyptians; I love looking at Egyptian paintings, tombs, statues. I love science and scientific reading. I quite like domestic things too, like making marmalade, building boats and gardening. I love taking part in poetry and music performances.'

Despite what some of her poems seem to suggest, her duties as wife and mother were not inimical to writing first-class poetry. On the contrary, everyday domesticity engendered some of her most frequently discussed poems, such as 'In the Park'. Its protagonist, a young mother sitting in a park while 'Two children whine and bicker, tug her skirt' and 'A third draws aimless patterns in the dirt', encounters a former lover, who looks pitifully askance at what she has become with marriage and motherhood. When he has gone, she contemplates her children and, as she nurses her youngest child and sits staring at her feet, realises 'They have eaten me alive.'

To those who believed the woman to be Gwen herself, she had a quick and cutting retort: 'You can't attribute those sayings to me. I'm always being accused of saying things that are said by my characters, as if I were some kind of Iago. I'm a *dramatic poet*; I create character; that's what gives the poetry some of its edge. People attribute those characteristics to me and ask my children, "Didn't your mother love you?"' She was firm about that too. 'I was completely enchanted with the children,' she said. 'I loved them so much.'

Gwen also wrote memorably about friends and friendship. Among the friends celebrated in verse were Rex Hobcroft, Jan Sedivka, A.D. Hope, and James McAuley. She published her first book of poetry in 1963 and her last in 1995. Her fifth, *Bone Scan*, won her the Victorian Premier's Literary Award in 1989 and the National Poetry Award the following year.

Like the English poet Phillip Larkin, whose work she admired, Gwen Harwood wrote poetry that does not have to be solved like a cryptic crossword. 'It's hard to convince people that the poems are meant for human enjoyment,' she said, 'not objects of study.'

Despite the variety of topics she wrote about with insight (and often with wry humour), her ability to hauntingly evoke the natural world of Tasmanian landscape and climate is something that makes her work stand out. Take, for example, her description of 'Springtime, Oyster Cove':

> Springtime returns, old love thought lost
> and found by chance. The hillside lapses
> from its strict tones of cold to sweetness.
> Wildflowers illuminate their names:
> white iris, scorpion everlasting,
> lilac bells, speedwell, waxflower, musk.
> Seabirds possess their field of blue,
> songbirds their bowl of milky sky.
> Sapphire, turquoise, pastoral
> viridian on the hills of Bruny.
> Everything's occupied with life,
> thrusting, relentless, fountaining
> with sap and hope.

To Tasmanian eyes and ears, that lyrical juxtaposition of water and land epitomises the island landscape we know and love so well. It is Romantic poetry, and Gwen Harwood was quite content to be considered a Romantic. Yet despite her accomplishments she remained modest about her work. 'I don't think of myself as a poet,' she said. 'You're only a poet if you've written a few very good poems, a few poems that will stay. Perhaps none of mine will; you can't tell. You've only got to pick up one of the great English poets and read for a while to feel utterly humbled.'

Gwen Harwood died in December 1995, leaving an artistic gap – and, to her many friends and acquaintances, a personal one. A warm, witty woman with restless hands, a quick and purposeful walk, and erudite stream-of-consciousness talk, she was one whom it was a joy to bump into and engage in conversation on a city street or in Christopher Pearce's Hobart Bookshop, her favourite. Though often seemingly in a hurry, she admitted that she loved to chat. 'I think I like idle talk best of everything in life – just talking to friends. If there's one thing I'd really like to have in Heaven, it's idle talk.'

She, like her poetry, reflected her love of life. 'I have always loved the world,' she said. 'I have an absolute passion for its delights. I live in the world of which Wittgenstein said, "Nothing can correspond to my wonder at the world."'

# An Unforgettable Educator

## Gae Williams

On 18 November 1994, Gwen Harwood honoured the Grade 4/5 students at South Hobart School with a visit. What a privilege it was to have such an amazing guest! A person of such integrity with an overwhelming presence, she talked with my students, she listened to them, she shared with them. She talked of the harmony and understanding of the natural world, her thoughts about love and loss, life and death, caring for the environment and its sustainability. She was inspirational!

The classroom became almost a hallowed place where the children were able to express their thoughts openly and without fear. Gwen's enthusiasm and enthralling use of words, along with her total honesty and genuine caring, encouraged the most amazing writing from this group of students. Children who had never written a poem before began to play with words with fun and feeling – a miracle! They loved Gwen's poem 'Twilight', feeling that they knew her beloved cat Mr Gabriel Fur intimately. Her sense of humour was infectious and rather unique.

The children wrote of their feelings in their thank-you letters to Gwen and incredibly she wrote back to each one of them – personal letters full of charm and wisdom. Many of those letters are held as treasures to this day.

The memory of this brilliant poet will live on in her writing but very special memories will be held in the hearts of all present that Friday at South Hobart School. When Gwen Harwood left us, the room seemed suddenly so silent. She had the power to make me laugh, cry and feel tortured, yet feel so intimately about the idiosyncrasies of life.

# Poet and Paradox

## Janet Upcher

When I think about Gwen now, I realise how elusive she was, and how rare.

She could be tough and tender, caustic and sweet, cynical and accepting all at once. To me, Gwen was a paradox. Her sharp mind made it impossible for her to waver from a well-considered opinion, or a point of view substantiated by reason, yet at the same time she could express blind faith in intuition and come to conclusions informed entirely by emotion. These contradictions within her personality are probably what made her poetry so powerful, what gave it tension and unpredictability. The toughness of mind and ideas expressed in her words was always softened by an emotional depth and musicality in metre, mood and rhythm. She could have been a great philosopher or a great musician, but fortunately for us she combined both talents in remarkable poetry instead.

Gwen had a talent for kindness. I remember especially a writers' forum where many luminaries were gathered. It was quite soon after the death of my mother, with whom Gwen had formed a fond friendship. She knew that I was grieving and distressed and at the end of the panel discussion, when she was greatly in demand for lunch, she turned down all invitations and insisted that I join her for a chat. This was typical of Gwen's empathy and generosity of spirit.

Her wit and her mischievous sense of humour could be devastating if one were the target of her scorn. Scathing realism was often matched with girlish romanticism: her correspondence in the collection *Blessed City* demonstrates how her withering perceptions were often suppressed under a semblance of decorum. This was particularly apparent when she saw through sometimes arrogant and pretentious attitudes within academe, also when she suspected fawning and obsequiousness among admirers.

It was impossible for Gwen to arrive empty-handed when invited somewhere. I remember her turning up often on the doorstep laden, like little grey rabbit, with baskets of produce lovingly harvested from her garden or, like her ruby-red crab apple jelly, created in her kitchen. Gwen was a connoisseur of food and an excellent cook and hostess. Even when she was most ill, she would insist that visitors stay for 'a sandwich or soup' and 'a glass of something'.

Her kindness was boundless. She loved giving small gifts to bring pleasure to children and loved the pleasure brought by animals (especially cats) and birds. She knew the distinctive calls of many birds and was enchanted by birdsong. She loved fishing too but was conflicted over the killing of flathead.

When I contemplate Gwen Harwood's international reputation as a brilliant poet, one of Australia's foremost female writers, it's often hard to reconcile that public image with the other Gwen, the motherly, kind-hearted, down-to-earth practical woman who always put others' needs before her own and who loved a wicked laugh.

As do so many others, I miss her. I loved and admired her warmth and valued her wisdom. Thanks to her enduring legacy of words, though, she's never far away.

# The Sweet Singer of Pine Street

## Don Kay

I first knew of Gwen Harwood in 1965, through her collaboration with composer Larry Sitsky, as librettist for his one-act opera *The Fall of the House of Usher*. This was one of three one-act operas composed specially for performance during the second National Conference of Australian Composers that year. The performances all took place one evening in Hobart's Theatre Royal. I was fresh back from London, where I'd lived since 1959, to take the newly created position of Lecturer in Music at Hobart's Teachers' College, my first job in my home state. My anticipation had been, I must confess, of a fairly arid musical scene. Both the conference and the mini festival of brand-new Australian operas, especially Larry and Gwen's creation, did much to allay my apprehensions about returning to Hobart.

I don't recall actually meeting Gwen till 1971, during the Festival of Tasmania, for which I composed and arranged music for *The Cycle of Wakefield Plays*, directed by Diana Large. The whole cycle took three consecutive evenings. My meeting then with Gwen was at one of those City Hall evenings. Her well-established reputation caused me to feel a little inhibited, but her genuine warmth and lack of any pretension somewhat eased those feelings every subsequent time I met her. When we began to work together, this sense of inhibition was replaced by an increasing sense of awe. She had such a way with words, producing her wonderful texts, either libretti or poetry for music setting, with such speed and seeming ease and spontaneity that I was continually astonished. Furthermore, when she wrote to me (her most frequent mode of communication) to do with one of our projects, she often signed herself 'your humble servant' or 'your servant, as ever' and once, 'the sweet singer of Pine Street'.

In her collaborations with composers, Gwen always considered herself a servant of the composer, whereas I believed the collaboration should be on equal terms. She pleaded with me a number of times to allow her to redo things if I found anything at all unsatisfactory. I can honestly say I tried very hard to find fault with her texts, really to convince her as well as myself that I had sound judgemental capacities. The only 'fault' I could find with the libretto for our one-act opera *The Golden Crane*, for example, was an over-wordy scene one, for my purposes. Within a week, a newly pruned scene one arrived in the post. Her words, specially written for music setting, were so right for me. She claimed she could hear my music, in advance, dictating the words for her. I found that quite astonishing. She accepted my music to her words with never a negative comment, except, perhaps, on just one occasion. In 'Petroglyphs', a movement of our choral suite *Northward the Strait*, she suggested I use a nineteenth-century Anglican hymn tune she referred me to, with her words, to represent European settlers in Van Diemen's Land in conflict with the Aborigines, rather than the music I'd composed. I readily complied.

Gwen seemed to have a special affinity with musicians. She refers to music, performers and composers often in her poetry and wrote poems dedicated to some she knew personally. One such was Rex Hobcroft, her long-time friend and both pianist and occasional composer. He once said to me that he believed Gwen fell a little in love with each of the composers she was collaborating with at the time. Her generosity was immense, with ideas and suggestions offered in relation to our projects. She was a prolific sender of postcards and letters. She nearly always selected cards relevant to the topic of our project. All the cards she sent me relevant to *The Golden Crane* (which was based on a Japanese folk tale), for example, were of charming Japanese images, except the last. She apologised for that being Chinese because she had exhausted her Japanese supply.

For our fourth and final work together, *Song of Welcome*, commissioned for the 1990 opening ceremony of the International Rowing Festival at

Lake Barrington in northern Tasmania, she dashed off several poems (accompanied by 'rowing' cards), inviting me to select the poem I most preferred. I can't say what she did with those rowing poems I didn't require, but I still have them.

Gwen seemed not to mind too much if her words weren't projecting audibly enough during performances of her opera libretti. She very generously said to me once that it was sufficient for her to realise her words had inspired the music she was hearing. She certainly became very emotionally involved in performances of our work together. I can recall at least three occasions during three different works, *The Golden Crane*, *Northward the Strait*, and *The Waking of the World*, when I was sitting next to her in the audience. I glanced across at particular moments and noticed tears streaming down her cheeks. Such moments touched me unbelievably.

For our third collaboration, Gwen and I were commissioned by the Mersey Valley Festival of Music Inc., supported by the Australian Bicentennial Authority, to create a work for the Australian Bicentenary in 1988. The brief was to create a work for mixed chorus, soloists and concert band. It also had to be about Tasmania's northwest region and no more than twenty-five minutes' duration. Gwen, as ever, thoroughly researched the area and identified geological features such as the Stanley Nut and hanging rock at Mount Roland. On a postcard in a shoebox in Sheffield, she found an 1890s photo of the rock, with three men posing nearby. She posted it to me with an accompanying humorous poem. (The rock, incidentally, has fallen long since.) Along with that poem and postcard, she sent (in quick time) five other poems concerned with a variety of aspects to do with the northwest region. I began work with great enthusiasm as that area was my personal area of origin and childhood. Gwen's opening words of the first movement of our choral suite began 'Northward the strait, with its hundred islands; westward the ocean, southward the mountains, and overall the cleanness of air polished by winds that circle the world.' That was enough to get me going, as those words seemed to immediately conjure up the spirit of the place in my imagination. I soon found that I'd never do justice to all six poems with the twenty-five-minute duration. I decided to cull two poems, much to Gwen's disappointment. I did promise her, however, that one day I'd add the other two poems and do a complete version using symphony orchestra as an alternative to the concert band. Sadly, Gwen became ill and died before this was achieved.

Around 2003 or 2004 an opportunity for performance arose. I finally had the incentive to add the outstanding poems to make a complete orchestral version, in anticipation. Unfortunately, that opportunity for performance faded but ironically, in 2008 I was asked for the original concert band version to be included in the 2009 Australian Intervarsity Choral Festival in Hobart. For that performance I also arranged the two outstanding poems for concert band to join the original four that Gwen had heard in a 1988 performance. The 2009 performance, now the complete work, involving the Intervarsity Festival Choir, Christopher and Amy Richardson (vocal soloists) and the Hobart Wind Symphony conducted by Simon Reade, was dedicated to the memory of Gwen Harwood. I have to say that in the lead-up rehearsal week, due to the awful flu epidemic, disaster threatened. Half the choir of 140 were struck down, and two days before the event Amy Richardson, vital as soprano soloist, also became ill. June Tyzack, chorus master, was forced to miss important rehearsals but rallied towards the end of the week. On the day of the performance, the choir mustered 100 voices, Amy rose heroically from her sickbed and miraculously the performance went ahead in a manner that would have done Gwen proud. This sentiment I conveyed to all the personnel involved following their grand performance at the UTAS Burbury Theatre, the same venue that Gwen had heard the 1988 version.

To complete the story of my collaboration with Gwen Harwood, I must mention two further projects, mooted but never proceeded with, like two unrealised bookends to begin and conclude our association. The first involved the Theatre Royal Light Opera Co., whose music director was Gwyneth Dixon. In the mid to late 1970s she called me on the telephone to ask if I'd care to write an opera for the company. I was quite startled by this request as I hardly knew Gwyneth and wasn't sure she would know of me. I don't remember whether I gave a decisive answer but I did contact Gwen

Harwood, whom I'd met once by this time. I was very tentative and shy in my approach, feeling a bit audacious. She was the only person in Hobart I knew of as a librettist and I had great admiration for that aspect of her work. Whatever transpired in that conversation I can't clearly remember. What resulted, though, and extraordinarily rapidly, was a many-pages-long draft for a libretto (on a subject entirely of Gwen's choosing) in the post something like a fortnight later. Sadly, nothing ever came of it as I never heard from Gwyneth again.

One of my very last contacts with Gwen, not long before her final illness, was in relation to another proposed project. I had recently read a very positive review of a book, a novel, I believe, to do with colonial sealers and adventurers in Bass Strait. I phoned her to express my interest in this book as a possible potential subject for a new work together, not realising she had just read the same review. She explained she was about to contact me with a similar proposal. That is an example of the compatibility of our working relationship. I never met her again even though I expressed a wish to do so, knowing how ill she had become. I heard she had no wish to see people during her final twelve months.

I will always remember certain particularities of Gwen's demeanour. She was quite short but not really diminutive, with an almost birdlike manner – always alert with quick, precise movements. If unexpectedly approached by an acquaintance at, say, a concert at interval, her first reaction, I noticed, was of a slightly startled look till recognition immediately transformed it into a warm, beaming smile of welcome that brilliantly lit up her whole personality. Her big, round, shining and intelligent eyes took in everything around her, darting around nervously, observing every nuance in the group of people she might be with. She seemed always ahead of the game and not given to small talk. I remember that if a silence fell in the conversation for any length, she sometimes had the disconcerting characteristic of suddenly turning away and whisking herself off, but not before she left the company with a summing up, a witty, poetic phrase that encapsulated the gist of the topic of conversation.

My final contact was a phone call to ask her permission to dedicate my second symphony, *The South Land*, to her, to which she agreed. During that brief conversation I had a strong sense of it being our final exchange, which I believe Gwen shared. As I put down the phone, I had a large lump in my throat.

# First Sight of the Famous Poet

## Tim Thorne

My first awareness of Gwen Harwood was through reading the famous acrostic in *The Bulletin*. Somebody must have alerted me to its hidden message, as I, an earnest teenager who took all things poetical with extreme (and often unwarranted) gravity, would never have thought of looking for it.

Very soon afterwards I enrolled at the University of Tasmania and my own versifying efforts found me on a stage alongside Jim McAuley, presenting a program that consisted of readings from the works of Gwen and of Vivian Smith, as well as his and mine. I am not sure why Gwen was not reading her own poems, but I vaguely remember being told that she was too shy to do so. On getting to know her later, I had strong doubts as to the veracity of that as a reason. Her non-participation was certainly not due to her being away somewhere, something I discovered to my mortification as the audience assembled and there she was, centre of the front row.

The expectation of the reception deserved by a mere undergraduate who, minimally published and giving his juvenilia their first public airing, should presume to present Gwen Harwood's works alongside his own, disconcerted me, to state the least. I was acutely conscious of how brash I must have appeared. I was even more acutely conscious of her face, outwardly smiling but, I was sure, with a smile that masked thoughts critical, if not scornful, of my efforts. I can no longer remember which of Gwen's poems I read, but I shall never forget the faux pas that followed my reading of the first of them. Some combination of confusion and lack of confidence took over the part of my brain responsible for speech, and I asked Gwen if she had anything to add concerning the poem. As if she hadn't said, and said magnificently, all there was to say by using the words that were there on the page! She graciously replied in the negative, with a soft voice and a slight shake of the head.

Other really vivid memories of Gwen arise from her phenomenal ability to create witty verse at short notice. She won the Poetry Ashes at the Circular Head Arts Festival in 1989, but it was her performance in the Launceston Poetry Cup as part of the 1991 Tasmanian Poetry Festival that showed this ability at its highest level. After all the entries had been presented, there was a short break while the judges conferred and punters refreshed themselves. The announcement of Gwen as the winner came as no surprise. She was scheduled to read a bracket of poems immediately after the awarding of the cup. The first poem she read was a response to her victory. There are three possibilities. Either she had composed this piece while actually in the process of receiving the trophy (a time measured in seconds rather than minutes), she was extemporising rather than reading or, with supreme confidence, she had prepared it beforehand. Unfortunately, as is the case with many of her occasional poems, no copy of any of these pieces seems to be in existence. Gwen always made a clear distinction between these, intended as ephemeral, and her poems 'for publication'.

# A Culinary and Literary Artist

## Alison Hoddinott

I first met Gwen Harwood on a chilly autumn evening in 1952 when, as a twenty-year-old research assistant to her husband, Bill, a senior lecturer in the English Department at the University of Tasmania, I was invited to their house in Augusta Road, Lenah Valley. Ostensibly, the visit was to discuss the progress of my research, but, more importantly, it was to meet his wife, who wrote poetry, some of which had been published in journals like *Meanjin* and *The Bulletin*. I remember that, on that evening, Gwen had a German dictionary propped on the shelf above the kitchen sink, that she complained of the Tasmanian cold and that she was pregnant with the twins, Peter and Mary, who would be born later that year.

In many ways, Gwen was a surprise. I was accustomed to Bill Harwood's probingly rational approach to academic questions. Gwen was far more impulsive, intuitive and mercurial. The evening conversation ranged widely, from German lyrical poetry to the complexity of English suffixes. At ten o'clock Gwen produced tea and cinnamon toast. Her own recollection of our first meeting included the detail that she was making plum jam at the time. It was the first of many similar visits to the house in Augusta Road before my departure for England in September 1954.

From the outset and beyond a shared love of poetry, our friendship was based on domesticity and female experience. Although I did not know it at the time, Gwen had met my mother in 1946 in the maternity ward of Calvary Hospital. Gwen's first child, John, and my mother's sixth and last child, Janet, were both born in August of that year. According to Gwen, my mother told her that her own children had been the source of great delight to her and that she was sure Gwen was about to discover similar pleasures in motherhood. A continuous line of childbearing was to link our families, as my own first child, Anne, was born in England in 1956 and was therefore only four years younger than the Harwood twins.

When I returned to Hobart in November 1957 with my husband and my year-old daughter, we became firm friends of the Harwoods. My husband (also Bill) was appointed to a temporary lectureship in the English Department and thus he became a colleague of Bill Harwood. During our two years in Hobart, there were frequent five o'clock sherries, Sunday lunches and evening visits. In a letter to us in 1962, Gwen wrote nostalgically,

> I see Easter is late this year; I never think of it without remembering those Good Friday hot-bun sessions, Al, and wish we were in the same city with hot buns or beer and sausage rolls or chokky bikkies or anything.

At the beginning of 1960, we moved with our now two daughters to the University of New England in Armidale, northern New South Wales. On summer holiday returns to Hobart, our visits to the Harwoods were always the source of enormous pleasure. On one occasion that first year, we went on a picnic with Gwen and Bill to Dover and Hasting Caves. We left our children with my mother and the Harwood children with Gwen's grandmother and enjoyed a blissful day of freedom in which we swam in the thermal pool at Hastings and ate a lunch of chicken legs, bread rolls, fruit and Christmas cake. Gwen later wrote a sonnet that read acrostically 'The Thermal Pool', which she included in a letter in which she remembered our eating 'chook legs down by Garden Island Creek'.

I have written elsewhere of my recollections of Gwen as *Bulletin* hoaxer, originator of literary pseudonyms, manufacturer of Sappho cards and, above all, as a gifted poet. But on rereading the letters she wrote to us in the early 1960s before the publication of her first volume of poetry, I am struck by the frequency of the references to domesticity and to food and drink.

The sausage rolls we enjoyed at Easter were not the shop-bought variety. Gwen made her own and was aware of our admiration for this skill. She signed one of her letters 'your favourite sausage-roll-supplier, Gwen

Harwood', and in another predicted that friends who had displeased her would, in future, 'find the sausage rolls a bit cold'. When Anne started school in 1962, I found that I would be required to bake cakes for a patty cake day. Embarrassed by my lack of competence in producing these delectable items, I wrote to Gwen and, by return mail, received a recipe that lay in my kitchen folder for many years. Gwen's instructions began,

> – here's all you do:
> Into one large bowl put
> 1½ cups flour (S.R.)
> ½ cup milk
> 2 eggs
> ½ cup caster sugar
> 1 teaspoon vanilla essence
> 4 ozs soft butter or margarine

Beat hell out of this until it's all mixed smooth; if it's too stiff to beat thoroughly, add more milk or if you are madly extravagant another egg. It should be firm, not runny. Two-thirds fill patty cake papers and bake 10 mins at 400 degrees. If the batter looks uninteresting to the local connoisseurs add some currants or sultanas. If I am in a hurry I melt the butter; it doesn't seem to make any difference.

Gwen's letter concluded, 'Sometimes my cakes are quite horrible too, Al, don't let it get you down. If they seem to be quite inedible I roll them in coconut after dipping them all over in thin wet icing; kids eat this… Have a nice patty cake day.'

Family birthdays are celebrated 'with the feast crudely known as "chook and cake" by the children'. The Harwoods go on picnics to the Botanical Gardens ('Tongue sandwiches, beer and chocolate crackles; what more could anyone want?') or up the Lenah Valley Track to the Springs on the side of Mount Wellington bearing asparagus sandwiches, beer, chocolate and sausages to be grilled on a stick. She notes with alarm the increasing appetites of her children, remarks on her popularity with the butcher, and signs off one letter with 'Well, like I said, off to roast the tender rolled and boned shoulder.'

Sometimes she complains ironically that the demands of looking after the family limit her poetic creativity and she longs for some quiet time to herself. On a picnic to the Salmon Ponds in the Derwent Valley, she is struck by the peaceful setting and feels that she could write 'an epic, if left there with a pie and Thermos'. On another occasion, busy preparing meals for the family, she wishes to be left alone with 'a loaf of bread, jug of wine (on a tray) so I can write a few masterpieces'.

Descriptions of social occasions to welcome visitors to the English Department frequently include details of the food and drink enjoyed (or not). In the early 1960s, Gwen, who had already won poetry prizes and had her work published in literary magazines, met a number of established poets and academics, some of whom later became her firm friends. One of those was James McAuley. In her letter about the McAuleys' first meal at 89 Augusta Road ('baked trumpeter and pineapple meringue'), she was pleased to see his enjoyment of the food she had cooked ('he said "Wonderful" and went for it like a dog') and feared she had not given him enough ('next time I'll give him a bit more fish on his plate'). On the other hand, when she prepared roast duck and jellied pears for Vincent Buckley, she was disappointed that he played with his duck, ate sparingly of the jellied pears and refused the claret. At a lunch given by Norma and James McAuley to welcome the visiting English poet John Betjeman, 'the food was beyond belief: fabulous things in jellies, MOUNTAINS of asparagus…a gigantic strawberry confection with alps of cream'. When Vivian and Sybille Smith gave an evening party for Professor Leonie Kramer, Gwen admired Sybille's production of 'a marvellous glorious Austrian cake with cream and toffee incorporated in it'.

Sometimes, however, the food provided on social occasions is truly horrible or non-existent. At lunch with Ann Jennings at the Ship Hotel, they were given, at enormous cost, 'tough chicken, mushrooms that looked like and tasted of cow-shit and peas like petrified finches' eggs'. At an evening to meet Australian composers given by the Adult Education Board, the food and drink were so scanty that, by 10.15, 'people were sucking the juice out of the dahlias'.

When we moved to Armidale in early January 1960, we must have written about the warmth of summer in the northern New South Wales city and the abundance of tropical fruit. We had bought a bucket of oranges for a shilling! From then on, that bucket of oranges became a recurrent motif in letters in which Gwen lamented the chilly greyness of the southern capital.

Bill Harwood's garden in Augusta Road produced masses of the kind of fruit and vegetables that flourish in Tasmania and Gwen enthusiastically reported that they were enjoying beans, sweet corn, strawberries and red currants. She made splendid jams and jellies from the garden fruit, but the more exotic oranges did not always succeed:

> Damn all marmalade…some of it seems to be turning into a kind of liqueur, fermenting anyway.

After Bill Harwood retired and the children left home, the Harwoods moved to a small property near Kettering in the D'Entrecasteaux Channel and overlooking the Bruny Island ferry's point of departure. Gwen named the place Halcyon after the mythical bird supposed to breed at the winter solstice and to calm the winds and waves. We enjoyed many days of windless calm on our summer visits to Halcyon. We ate magnificent lunches and went on exploratory walks, while the men went fishing in *Sappho*, the latest boat built by Bill Harwood. One afternoon we all took a walk along the foreshore to Oyster Cove and found we were going through a deserted orchard. One of the trees was covered with purple damson plums which we gathered in our hats. The next day, Gwen presented us with a pot of damson jam labelled Ceres and inscribed with the date and the place of gathering. She commented that she hated to waste any of the fruits of nature. It was an attitude characteristic of both her poetry and her life.

# Madam President

## Wal and Berenice Eastman

Hobart members of the Fellowship of Australian Writers used to meet at a place quite redolent with literary atmosphere – The Elms in North Hobart, where even the tea trolley seemed to have its own mythology. Foremost in our minds were memories of nine wonderfully enriching residential seminars, no fewer than five of which were held at Waddamana up in the high lake country above Bothwell, where workshops were given by such renowned guest speakers as Dorothy Porter, Barney Roberts, Gary Disher and Tim Thorne.

It was an exciting adventure to arrive up there on a cold evening after the long drive out to Bothwell, then up into the mountains, to arrive at last at the historical old power station hostel. Through the big windows of the lounge room we travellers could see the writers who had already arrived. There was the reassuringly familiar figure of our beloved president, Gwen Harwood, in her customary striped woolly jumper, sitting in the midst of a cheerful company enjoying steaming mugs of cocoa or coffee in front of a roaring fire. These occasions drew a stimulating company of people from the northwestern and northern branches of FAW Tas, as well as from our southern one.

On another occasion we were bound for Deloraine, where we were booked into the premises of a fundamentalist Christian group in Golden Valley. Comforts were rather sparing in this very inexpensive domicile. Their lack caused one of our guest speakers to hie herself urgently into town for a quick purchase of something more fortifying at the local pub, and on her return to deplore vociferously the lack of warmth in this Christian retreat. It should be entered into the annals of Tasmanian literary history that Gwen Harwood, no less, took it on herself to seek out the boiler in the lower regions of this Golden Valley hostel and successfully do battle with it, eventually to establish peace and comfort above stairs.

Berenice Eastman

She looked like everybody's grandmother, but behind that benign round face was a piercing intellect and a peerless ability to use words.

The Gwen Harwood we knew at All Saints Church, Hobart, was our organist and a member of the parish council – able, affectionate and musical.

The Gwen we knew as former president of the Fellowship of Australian Writers was creative, innovative and always – *always* – helpful and encouraging to new writers. She presided over our monthly meetings with genial authority and wit, and advanced the standing of the FAW in the Tasmanian cultural community.

It was a privilege and the greatest of fun to be present at an art exhibition, a book launch or any other function she opened because it was inevitably done in verse – and not just some patched-together doggerel but very entertaining poetry.

This great Australian poet, who received honours and recognition on the world stage, embodied a unique blend of poise, humility and humour. She was able on one hand to receive the Governor or the Lord Mayor at the beginning of a meeting and afterwards to wield a broom to help clean the hall.

Towards the end, she had her share of pain, and in her last postcard to my wife and me, after referring to a Handel organ piece she loved to play, 'Angels, waft her to the skies' from *Jephta*, added, 'How I wish they would!'

Well, they have – and we continue to miss her terribly.

Wal Eastman

# The Golden Wine of Rest

## Stephen Edgar

It hardly seems credible, I know, but it was not until I was in my thirties that I caught my first fish. This delayed rite of passage occurred in the company of Gwen Harwood, sometime in the mid-1980s, as we sat in her dinghy far out in Oyster Cove, south of Hobart, in the middle of a Sunday afternoon, hearing and feeling the slap of the wavelets against the sides of the boat. Ann Jennings, the third member of the crew, was recalling fishing expeditions of her youth and the dispatch of gasping flathead by a single blow of an implement known in her family as a bodger. This led to speculation on the capacity of fish to feel pain. Gwen capped the conversation with a fantasy about a giant Old Man Flathead on the bed of the bay who might rise to the dinghy and pluck us all to our deaths, reassuring his fellow flathead with the words, 'Don't worry. They can't feel pain.' We pulled fish on board at a great rate before going back to Halcyon, Gwen's house at Oyster Cove, to skin and fillet them. One of the least of the things for which I should feel gratitude to Gwen Harwood, perhaps. But perhaps not. Such occasions are the stuff of life and of art.

On another occasion that Ann and I were visiting Gwen at Halcyon, she immediately dashed to the cassette player and put in a cassette. 'Listen to this,' she said. It was always Gwen's habit, particularly during her years at Oyster Cove, but also in West Hobart where she spent the last years of her life, to greet the arriving guest with a cargo of the latest books she had read, records she was listening to, letters and photographs she had received from children and friends. This could be a dizzying experience as one's attention was drawn from one object to another, but for this very reason, fortunately, a considered critical response was not often called for. Soon enough you would be whisked out of your seat and taken on a tour of the property, or fed like a king, or rather both. 'I was in the kitchen preparing lunch,' she went on, 'when this song started, and it took me a few seconds before I tuned in to it and realised I was listening to a masterpiece.' As a result, the opening verses of the song were missing. It was called, I think, 'The Ballad of Jacob and Marcie', or something like that; I can't remember the name of the performers. Towards the end, Marcie, an evil seductress, sings,

> You gave your soul to Jesus, Jacob,
> But your body belongs to me.

The song then concludes,

> She was slender as a willow,
> She had golden angel hair,
> But the Devil must have made her by hand.

I don't recall Gwen ever mentioning or playing the tape again. Years later, when her last book, *The Present Tense*, appeared not long before her death in 1995, I was struck by these words in the poem 'This Artifice of Air':

> Your wits belong to Wittgenstein
> but your body belongs to me.

And I wonder whether it is completely coincidental that one of the two characters in the poem is called Golden Child. The adjective 'golden' would have a particular personal significance for Gwen, of course, for reasons I will come to later, and which may explain why she took those lyrics so much to heart. And the figure of a bright-haired girl who seemed angelic but was actually demonic bears some resemblance to her own retrospective depictions of herself as a child.

When remembering Gwen Harwood, one of the things that come tautologically to mind is memory itself. Memory, of course, was one of the central and most obsessive themes of her poetry and, in her later years, of many of those prose pieces that restored, word perfect, one might say, scenes from her childhood. And this brings us to the second sense in which memory summons memory, for Gwen herself had the most prodigious of memories, as anyone who knew her even moderately well can attest.

What was it about Gwen and memory? Some of her prose accounts of her childhood contain scraps of song and verse recited to her by her parents or grandmother, and I don't know whether I am correct in speculating that those words, faithfully recorded decades later, had not been seen or heard by Gwen since her childhood, but I wouldn't be at all surprised. Of course, a well-trained memory, particularly one trained in childhood, has an extraordinary capacity, and she had a powerful incentive for keeping that memory in trim. In all her writing life, she never had a room of her own to write in. Like Jane Austen, she had only the dining table to work on, when it was free, and consequently much of her composition was done in her head.

Almost any song or poem, or literary reference of any kind, that came up in the course of conversation would be likely to elicit from her a quoted line or stanza or sentence without a moment's hesitation. I remember the poet Andrew Sant telling me on one occasion how he had been chatting to Gwen and had mentioned in passing a song by Neil Young, not a singer Gwen might be expected to be specially familiar with. Not only did she know the song in question, she proceeded to rattle off all its lyrics, to Andrew's considerable astonishment. We often hear, and even perhaps repeat, the view that no experience is ever completely lost to the human mind, that somewhere in the brain, in some neural safe or vault, everything we have known is stored, if only we could retrieve it. Of Gwen Harwood you sometimes felt that here was a woman who had found the key to achieve just that feat.

Certainly the memorable in poetry was of the utmost importance to her, and she would often deliver sharp-tongued dismissals of what she considered the slipshod and forgettable products of one or another figure on the contemporary poetry scene. So highly developed was her capacity to commit to memory almost anything that was metrically amenable to it that once, when I was interviewing her for *Island* magazine, I made the mistake of touching on this subject by asking her something like 'By memorable, do you mean memorisable?' There was a moment's pause, as though I had caught her off guard, before she snorted a dismissive expletive.

Perhaps in her case, memorising was not the problem. She may have been somewhat like that character Funes, in the Borges story, who was incapable of forgetting, whose recall was so total that in order to review the events of a day he would require a day. It is the loss of memory that most of us fear; an excess of it might be just as fearful. It is well known that Gwen looked back on her childhood years in and near Brisbane as a time of bliss, a paradise on Earth. This was no mere sentimental nostalgia, however, she being only too well aware of death's presence in Arcadia. But in the same way that she could look back on those lost years and infuse them with radiance in her poetry, so could she do the same with the merest occasions of friendship. A day, an afternoon, an hour spent in Gwen's company, however enjoyable, might well be recalled to you by her at a subsequent meeting, bathed in so radiant an aura of fond recollection that you stood astonished at the transfiguration of the scene and your part in it, taking renewed pleasure in the occasion presented to you for a second glimpse, and yet feeling slightly unworthy for the poverty of your own imagination and emotions in comparison with hers. In such cases, it was as though the present functioned more as raw material for later recall than for its own sake. Of course, all writers are guilty of a similar sin, of using the lived life as the raw material of their art. But in her case I sometimes felt that this privileging of memory over the present was as much for her private use as for her poetry.

Despite the regular church attendance that marked her later years, I never got the impression that Gwen believed, as James McAuley evidently did, in the resurrection of the flesh and the redemptive power of Christ's blood. No, she was quite clear that the only immortality any of us can hope for is in the minds of those who remember us when we are gone – or indeed when we are still here but separated by the years or the wide world. I think of the early poem 'Anniversary' with its three stanzas, each ending with the appeal *remember me*. Now that she has gone, now that she has forgotten herself, as it were, we who remember her are also, curiously, remembering her memories, in so far as they reside in her work. The idea, I think, would appeal to her. She admired a good memory in others.

I wrote of the significance to her of 'golden'. When Vikram Seth first came to Australia, they met at the Adelaide Festival. He had published his celebrated novel *The Golden Gate*, written in the intricate and difficult stanza of Pushkin's *Eugene Onegin*. Gwen too was beginning to write in that form. They immediately hit it off together anyway, but that shared passion for a particular verse form was an additional bond. On the last day, different engagements meant they had not had the opportunity to say goodbye. Their paths just failed to cross. Gwen left an impromptu farewell Pushkin stanza for him. When she returned later, she found that he had already departed, leaving for her a stanza of his own, which he must have penned on the spot. It concluded,

> May the square flagons we love best Foster the golden wine of rest.

Gwen's maiden name was Foster, and 'golden wine of rest' is an anagram of Gwendoline Foster that she had devised in childhood. She had mentioned this to Seth during some dinner conversation that touched on anagrams. At that last moment, he had remembered her words and worked them into his valedictory verse.

I have many memories of Gwen, but perhaps the most intense are those from the period she lived at Oyster Cove, by the shore of the D'Entrecasteaux Channel, with views across to Bruny Island, the setting of many of her poems. I recall the superb, immaculately prepared and presented (and often too generous) meals, even down to the after-dinner chocolates invariably on hand, though Gwen herself disliked chocolate. I remember the guided tours around the property, with its geese and her beloved chooks, and the adjoining bush, and particularly the wonderful roll calls of plants and flowers that she would deliver in running commentary: white iris, scorpion everlasting, lilac bells, speedwell, waxflower, musk. She named them as we passed. I remember our walks around the shore of melancholy Oyster Cove, and that time out in the bay aboard the dinghy, hauling up the flathead, at the still centre of a Sunday afternoon, as the water and light, mimicking the eternal process, made a shaky mosaic of our reflections, which they unceasingly brought together and took apart.

# Demolition Dust and Doulton Cups

## Sarah Day

Any offerings I make to a book about Gwen Harwood will be anecdotal crumbs by contrast to the feast that those who knew her well will contribute. I have always greatly admired Gwen's poetry but I never knew her well. I was in my twenties and relatively new to writing poetry during the ten or so years that our paths crossed at readings and festivals in and out of Tasmania. At those brief encounters, she was kind and encouraging.

During the 1980s, the Tasmanian Writers Union ran a series of literary readings at Knopwoods Retreat in Salamanca Place. Gwen read there a number of times; it is at the podium by the fire of that historic building that I picture Gwen most vividly when remembering her. She had a beguiling and formidable manner of delivery, her gaze lifted sideways and upwards. As she recited her poems, often punctuating them with lengthy quotes by other authors, she appeared to be drawing the words from a source deep within and at the same time from an otherworldly muse. I remember her expression at such times as being both charged and angelic. Her remarkable, seemingly photographic memory was daunting to say the least.

Some time around what I recall as the end of 1991 or the beginning of 1992, when I was almost nine months pregnant with our first child, there was a knock at the door. Gwen Harwood, who was strolling about our mutual West Hobart neighbourhood with her friend Vikram Seth, had called to say hello. The north wall of our Georgian worker's weatherboard house was dismantled and mostly open to the elements; the plaster of many of the interior rooms had crazed and fallen off because the house was raised on truck jacks while it was being re-stumped. I invited my guests through the rubble to the kitchen to make a cup of tea, getting out the deco Doulton pansy cups by way of atonement for the dust and wreckage around them. I remember little of the conversation, only their mutual friendship and good humour.

Gwen left me on that somewhat surreal morning with an invitation to come, baby, pram and all, some weeks hence, for morning tea at her Pine Street house. Which I duly did. We talked about babies and about poetry. The gesture of her invitation was kindly, with perhaps a hint of empathy verging on sympathy. She knew better than I about what lay ahead for me – the strenuousness as well as the joy of early motherhood and the challenges of incorporating any sort of writing practice into this new life. She remembered the teacups and bestowed a present of a butter dish with pansies on the pram for the baby.

# Of Pseudonyms and Serendipity

## Robyn Mathison

I first discovered Gwen Harwood's poetry in the late 1950s in journals such as *Meanjin* and the annual Poetry Australia anthologies. The more of her work I read, the more I admired her. I didn't dream then that we would ever meet. In fact, it would be twenty years or so before I set eyes on her for the first time.

Meanwhile, one afternoon in 1961 a teaching colleague, who was also studying English at Adelaide University, told me that there were two very clever, very cheeky acrostic sonnets by Water Lehmann in the 5 August issue of *The Bulletin*. After work I rushed to the Mary Martin Bookshop in the city, bought a copy and leafed through it until I found the poems in the right-hand column on page 33: 'Eloisa to Abelard' and 'Abelard to Eloisa'. I chuckled as I read them and grinned when Max Harris commented that there had been a remarkable demand for this particular issue. Next day I heard that it had been withdrawn from sale across the county. Then in *The Bulletin* on 19 August I discovered that Walter Lehmann was none other than 'the Tasmanian housewife' poet Gwen Harwood. From then on, I checked all literary journals and books I could get my hands on, looking for Walter Lehmann's work as well as Gwen Harwood's.

When Angus & Robertson published Gwen's first poetry collection, *Poems*, in 1963, it contained a number of poems published originally under the Walter Lehmann pseudonym. Then in 1968 Gwen's three-part collection *POEMS/Volume Two* came out. The nineteen poems in Part 1 – including the wonderful Professor Kröte poems – had been published previously under the pseudonym Francis Geyer, whose work I'd already admired. In fact I'd kept my Autumn 1961 issue of *Quadrant* – as with that famous issue of *The Bulletin*, I still have it – purely on the strength of 'All Souls', the poem that opened that issue. The seven poems in Part 2 of *POEMS/Volume Two* had been published originally under the pen name Miriam Stone. Only the eighteen in Part 3 had been published previously under Gwen's own name.

Then in 1970 'Space Poem' by T.F. Kline was published in *Transition: An Australian Society of Authors Anthology* edited by Nancy Keesing. In the same year, Tom Shapcott included a biographical note the pseudonymous author supplied with three poems by Timothy Kline – 'Frog Prince', 'From a Young Writer's Diary' and 'Poet to Peasant' – in the Sun Books anthology *Australian Poetry Now*. I can't remember exactly when I discovered that Gwen Harwood was also Tiny Tim, but I marvelled at her ability to write with different voices for different pseudonyms, as well as for characters within the poems, such as the professors Eisenbart and Kröte.

Soon after I moved to Hobart in the mid-1970s and made contact with the local branch of the Fellowship of Australian Writers, I was delighted to find that Gwen Harwood was a member. When I first saw her, I found it hard to believe that this demure-looking woman could be the author of all that accomplished and often wickedly funny poetry I so admired. But then I had the chance to attend her readings and I saw the glint in her eyes and those occasional sardonic smiles.

Although at this stage I had met Gwen, I was still completely overawed by her and wondered if I'd ever get to know her. A visit from old friends made this possible. The Loftus family had been close friends in Adelaide, where Robin, a poet, had been active in the SA branch of FAW. In the late 1960s, the family moved to Newcastle, where Robin and her husband Pat, both psychologists, took up new jobs. Robin also joined the NSW Hunter Region branch of FAW and Jean and Norman Talbot soon became good friends. In the mid-1980s, Robin and Pat came to Hobart for a psychology conference and stayed with me. Norman Talbot had asked Robin to look up his great friend Gwen Harwood while she was here.

By then, the Harwoods had moved from Oyster Cove to West Hobart and when Robin asked me how she could make contact and get to see Gwen, I was able to tell her, 'That will be easy. She lives no more than a five-minute walk from here.' I plucked up enough courage to phone Gwen and arrange a meeting. On the day that other APS conference delegates were going off sightseeing, Robin and I strolled around to Pine Street, where Gwen greeted us warmly, gave us a quick tour of the garden and sat us down to morning tea. At first I sat quietly listening to Robin and Gwen speaking about Norman and other Newcastle poets they both knew, but when talk switched to FAW and more general talk of poetry I was able, very diffidently, to join in. That day marked the beginning of my friendship with Gwen and the first of many, many cups of tea at her kitchen table.

In 1989 Gwen became president of FAW Tasmania and the following year she co-opted me onto the committee as assistant to the secretary, Pat Barwick, who was ill. I worked closely with Gwen from then on, especially after I became secretary in 1991. In that year and the next, the Tasmanian FAW Executive was also the FAW Federal Council Executive. At branch committee meetings, we also had to conduct federal business and there was a lot of extra correspondence and other paperwork to do. Neither Gwen nor I had a computer in those days, but Gwen was a very fast and accurate typist and loved using her little electric machine. After she'd seen the ancient Imperial office typewriter I was using then, she volunteered to type much of the Federal Council correspondence, and we were back and forth a lot to each other's house, fetching and delivering FAW papers. At other times, too, Gwen often turned up at my place. 'Yoo-hoo,' she'd call and walk into the kitchen. 'I'm just out for a walk and I've come to Mary Street to see the chookies.' She'd often bring a pot of her home-made jam. At other times she'd bring a book or journal. She'd say, 'I don't want this back. Keep it, or pass it on.' She rarely came to my house empty-handed.

In March 1991, the three days of annual FAW Federal Council meetings were held at the Hobart Pacific Motor Inn. I saw Gwen in action by day presiding graciously and efficiently over the lengthy discussions, giving each delegate (all of them presidents of state branches) the chance to speak without letting anyone hog the floor. In the evenings, she made notes from memory of the day's proceedings to check later against the minutes I had taken. Gwen also helped organise a dinner at the hotel on the Saturday night so that FAW Tasmania committee members could meet the interstate delegates. At this dinner she gave one of her famous witty speeches-in-verse, which she always delivered from memory. For people not lucky enough to have heard any of these, some are published in *The Present Tense* (Sydney: Imprint, 1995), edited by Alison Hoddinott. They're well worth reading.

One morning later in 1991, working at my desk in the next room, I heard Gwen's voice in the kitchen saying, 'This is Charlotte and the other white-and-grey one is her son Charlie Fluff. The handsome black-and-white fellow is Nigel. The ginger tabbies are Tigger and his brother Tiger.' I walked into the room to find that Gwen was with a small man wearing a very large backpack and was introducing my cats to him. Without missing a beat she said, 'Ah, and here's my friend the FAW secretary, who lives with them.' And, turning to me, 'Robyn, I'd like you to meet Vikram Seth. I wanted him to see the Mary Street chookies – and to meet you too, of course.'

Gwen and Vikram Seth had met and discovered each other's work at Brisbane Writers' Festival in 1987 and they had been corresponding regularly since then. Seth had come to Australia again for a festival and he made a special trip to Hobart afterwards to see Gwen. She told me later, 'There's no room for guests at Pine Street. These days I book people in at the Marquis of Hastings. It's very handy, so easy to fetch them from there in the car and they can come to us for meals.' I'm sure Vikram Seth was very comfortable there. I also learnt that in the few days he was here she'd had Stephen Edgar visit to meet him and she had taken him to New Town to meet Anne and Giles Hugo and their family. Between visits to meet local writers and their cats and chooks and beagles, Vikram Seth and Gwen were also able to spend many hours at Pine Street, cooking, listening to music and talking.

In 1992 Gwen and I flew to Adelaide and stayed together at the Richmond Hotel in the city for three days of Federal Council meetings. Again, Gwen was businesslike and efficient chairing the meetings. In the evenings we'd compare notes on the day's proceedings and then join some of the other delegates for informal talk and dinner at a nearby Rundle Street restaurant. After the Council meetings ended, we were both able to stay on with family members for another three days so we could attend events at Adelaide Writers' Festival.

On the day we were booked to leave, at very short notice our flight from Adelaide was brought forward by three hours because baggage handlers at Melbourne airport were going out on strike later that day. We arrived at Tullamarine very early in the morning and Gwen suggested a stroll around the airport shops while we waited for our flight to Hobart to be called. Other early morning interstate flights were arriving every few minutes and most other passengers converging on the city were business people. Groups of them – men and women – kept appearing, all of them wearing dark suits and carrying attaché cases. As three large men approached, Gwen pulled me back into a shop doorway. 'Make way for the Important People, dear,' she said, not sotto voce. 'We mustn't make them late for their important meetings.' Then drawing me closer and giving one of her Cheshire-cat smiles, she rolled her eyes and inclined her head towards another group hurrying towards us. Two women wearing dark suits were struggling to keep up with a couple of men. The tapping of high heels echoed in the concourse as they tottered by. 'Look carefully, my kitten,' Gwen said. 'That's called power dressing. If you want to get on in the world, you'll have to get yourself a suit with dirty big shoulder pads.' She paused and said, more seriously, 'But I hope you'll wear sensible shoes.'

In the later 1980s Gwen served on both the Tasmanian and federal literature boards and by the 1990s she was in great demand to give readings or address meetings and was featured at many literary festivals. All this took up more and more of her time and energy, yet she managed to keep up correspondence with friends, among them dozens and dozens of other writers. She also continued her active involvement with FAW in Tasmania, giving many members written feedback on their writing. As well as attending the monthly general and committee meetings, she also attended the annual live-in workshop weekends for members. I recall that she was at Waddamana, Golden Valley and Dysart. In fact, at Golden Valley a couple of other Hobart women and I shared one of the bush cabins with Gwen.

In the little entrance foyer stood a tall cupboard on which a grey shrike-thrush had built a nest and was sitting on eggs. We were very careful not to disturb her when we went to bed quite late on the first evening. Next morning, when the dawn chorus began at the first glimmering of light in the bush outside, from her nest on the cupboard our shrike-thrush joined in. Pip-pip-pip-pip-jock-widd-ee, she called. As the deafening echo of the last sharply ascending syllable faded, out of the semi-darkness came Gwen's voice: 'Hands up those for birdsong!'

I loved Gwen's playfulness, her mercurial wit and her sense of humour – particularly her ironic response to anything pompous or pretentious. I also marvelled at her keen interest in just about everything under the sun and her prodigious memory. I grew to love her dearly, yet always remained very much in awe of her.

Even when we didn't work together as much after Gwen had stepped down as federal president and had become vice-president of FAW here, she continued to call in unannounced at my place fairly often. Early in our friendship she had said, 'Do call in whenever you're going to the Greeks'.' (This is what she always called the shop now known as the Hill Street Grocer.) So sometimes when I was going to the shop I'd gather a little nosegay of flowers or some fruit and I'd call on her. Often one of us would nurse the cat while we talked and drank tea. Occasionally Gwen would ask me to run some errand or telephone someone for her. As her final illness progressed, she made these simple requests more often. Gradually, though, in order not to tire her, I called in less often and my visits were much shorter. She always asked after the Mary Street creatures, what birds were about, what was in flower in local gardens and what mood the river was in that day. She still always said as I was leaving, 'Do come again soon. I need you to tell me what's happening in the world.'

Eventually one day Gwen telephoned to tell me that she had moved to St John's Hospital for palliative care. Only her family would be visiting. She would not be returning home. She did phone once more after that to ask me to do something for her but I didn't see her again until the night she died, when she came to me in a vivid dream and said goodbye.

On Sunday morning 4 February 1996, a group of writers and two young men from All Saints congregation – about a dozen of us altogether – held a littoral reflective gathering for Gwen at Silverwater Park, Woodbridge. In ones or twos we strolled along the water's edge for half an hour or so. As we gathered to sit together in a circle on the grass, a white-faced heron flew in from over the water. It settled in a tree near us and sat very still, with its head cocked in our direction. As we began to speak quietly, the bird flew down closer to us and perched on the railing of the footbridge over the rivulet. It stayed there, watching, while we ate our picnic lunch, shared memories of Gwen and read poetry. Only when we'd packed up our things and were heading towards the parked cars did the heron take off, flying low over the water towards Bruny Island.

Not long before this, I had a letter from writer Barney Roberts saying that he felt Gwen was still there, with all the birds, in the bush around his house at Flowerdale. On 7 February I wrote and told him about the littoral gathering and said that Gwen had been with us at Woodbridge on Sunday, too. I wrote, 'She will stay with us as long as memory lasts. How blessed we are to have known her – the kindness, the discerning eye, the wicked humour. The sadness is that she'll not visit again in person and that there will be no more of her new poems.'

# Dark Deeds and White Lace Collars

## Giles Hugo

In front of me as I write this, on the pinboard of my study wall, is a copy of the Tasmanian Writers Union Newsletter, mid-1993, featuring a photo I took of Gwen Harwood and a then-barely known travel writer (*From Heaven Lake: Travels Through Sinkiang and Tibet* [1983]) and poet (*The Golden Gate*, a novel in Onegin sonnets) who was soon to be a world-famous novelist as author of *A Suitable Boy*, Vikram Seth.

The picture was shot in early January 1992 in front of our grapevine, which will probably outlive us all. It is always sad when thinking back to those who have 'gone on', as some say. Gwen's death, after my knowing her for about eight years, did come as a shock, despite her age (seventy-five) and her previous encounter with cancer, so chillingly described in *Bone Scan* (1988).

That meeting with Vikram was thanks to Gwen. She had got to know him at the Adelaide Writers Festival and invited him to Tasmania. However, the accommodation booking was, fortunately for us, screwed up by the hotel, and Gwen asked if we would host Vikram for about six days. At the time, he had finished writing *A Suitable Boy*, which was in the process of being published, and he was travelling around with just a haversack and a shoulder bag, with probably half of what he carried being books.

Every day, Gwen would come over to visit Vikram, and they spent a great deal of time at our piano, with Gwen playing to accompany the duets they sang – mostly German lieder, some of which they had composed together. What a pleasure it was to hear and see two great sensibilities lighting up and pushing each other onward.

My wife, Anne Kellas, and I were privileged to get to know Gwen

*Vikram Seth and Gwen. (Photo: Giles Hugo)*

through poetry circles and various events, weekends and workshops she organised as Fellowship of Australian Writers president for several years in the late 80s and early 90s.

Gwen, the 'Hobart housewife' who scammed the phallocratic literati with her FUCK ALL EDITORS message hidden in plain sight, had a truly wicked wit. Several times at book launches or readings she would delight us with a terse barb relating to either the tedious launcher or reader, or whatever was being read – delivered in a meaningful whisper out of the corner of her mouth. I wish I had taken notes at the time.

And, despite her immaculate appearance and those white lace collars, she had some truly dark interests. When I was selling books at a stall at Salamanca market one Saturday, I noticed a small, intense lady sorting through my selection of horror stories and true crime. Mostly she was examining and putting aside anything relating to Jack the Ripper. 'Have you read this one?' I asked, picking out another gory Ripper title. Then I realised it was Gwen, and we spent a long time discussing Ripper theories – she seemed to know them all – with relish.

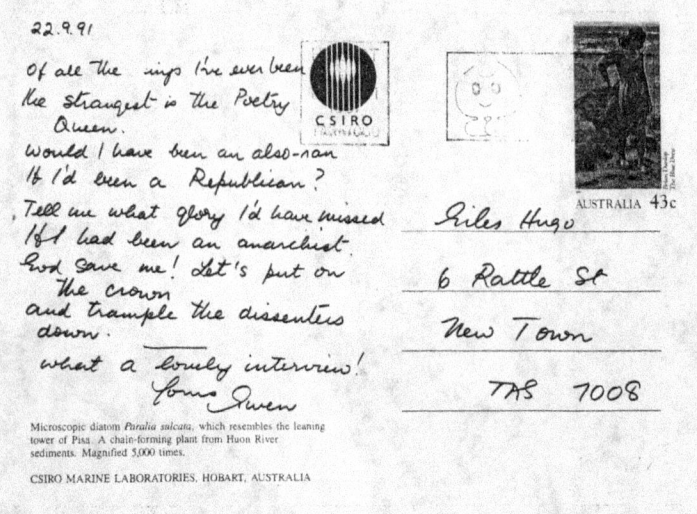

Her death was unexpected and shatteringly final for me. I heard that she had had to go back into hospital, but when I dropped in at her house with some flowers and a couple of books to be given to her, I was told by her family that she had died that day.

Strangely – to me – the funeral was private and there was no public memorial service. So, nearly twenty years later, I farewell Gwen Harwood, she of the twinkling eyes and barbed wit, passion for poetry and music, and immense kindness.

# Observer in the Chaucer Mould

## John Chilcott

There were, I suspect, few people outside the circle of All Saints Anglican Church, South Hobart, Gwen's family and her close friends who knew that Gwen was a very devout, pious, practising Anglican.

All Saints, the church Gwen attended, is the home of the Anglo-Catholic or High Church traditions in Tasmania and it follows orthodox Catholic doctrines and practices, but with an Anglican flavour. These traditions include elaborate ceremonies, such as High Masses, the teaching of the seven Sacraments (including the Sacrament of Confession), a belief in the centrality of the priesthood to the church's worship, the close observance of the traditional church calendar, the observance of saints' days, the honouring of the Virgin Mary, the wearing of vestments, processions, and the use of incense, shrines, candles and holy water. Gwen was a full participant in all these manifestations of Anglo-Catholic belief and customs. She attended Mass regularly, often on weekdays as well as Sundays, and participated in a wide range of the church's activities. She arranged flowers, she played the organ for services, she made cakes for morning teas and she was a member of a number of the church's groups.

A notable manifestation of Gwen's commitment to All Saints' orthodox, traditional form of Anglicanism was her membership of and active participation in the Confraternity of Our Lady of Walsingham, a group dedicated to the Virgin Mary and her apparition in 1061 at Walsingham in Norfolk.

Although Gwen was very devout, she was in no way sanctimonious or censorious in her faith; indeed, there was always a little hint of a smile or even a touch of wry humour attaching to her participation in the church's activities. This is not to say that she was at all frivolous or insincere, but she did sometimes give the impression that she was observing herself carrying out the church's observances. She was at once a participant and an appraising onlooker with a little twinkle in her eye. She seemed to regard All Saints and its parishioners with the same sharp-eyed but playful and kindly perspicacity that Chaucer did his pilgrims on their way to Canterbury.

Gwen's faith, kindness and humility were very evident at All Saints, and she was greatly admired and respected. Despite her great intellect, her extraordinary literary achievements and her fame, she saw herself and conducted herself as a simple parishioner who did God's work in simple parish activities. She mixed easily and cheerfully with a wide range of parishioners, irrespective of whether they were erudite, well-known, rich, unsophisticated, modest or poor. She conversed comfortably with all.

But Gwen certainly had a mind of her own and strong views on some parish matters.

In 1992, Father Alan Farrell was appointed parish priest of All Saints. In the months following his appointment, he became unpopular with some parishioners who disapproved of his behaviour both in the parish and outside. There were rumours of excessive drinking and bad behaviour in some of Hobart's public houses. There were, however, a number of parishioners who supported him, of whom Gwen was one.

In October 1993, Father Farrell was beaten by two men he had invited back to his North Hobart residence, bound with a necktie and placed in a bedroom cupboard. In 1994 he was charged with assault, aggravated assault and four counts of rape of a man at his (Father Farrell's) house. In July 1995 he was found guilty and sentenced to eight years' prison. In 1999 the High Court ordered a retrial, but the Crown decided not to proceed and Father Farrell was freed.

Unsurprisingly, the trial deepened the divisions in the parish between the supporters and the critics of Father Farrell. Gwen staunchly defended him from the beginning, and even more so during the trial. She became his close friend, supporter and frequent correspondent. Much of their correspondence, mainly that from Gwen, can be found in the Fryer Library of the University of Queensland.

Those events notwithstanding, Gwen continued as a faithful parishioner at All Saints until the end of her life. It should be added that although not all the parishioners supported her views on Father Farrell, Gwen was able to give her support openly without making a single enemy in the parish.

Gwen had a habit of adopting unlikely people as her friends and confidants. One of those at All Saints was Gerard Mocellin. Gerard was a French/Vietnamese man from Noumea in New Caledonia, who came to Hobart with his partner, John Chilcott, in 1985. Gerard was a Swiss-trained French chef who had no apparent educational or intellectual pursuits that matched Gwen's. She nevertheless saw something in him that took her fancy and soon took Gerard into captivity. In no time, they had established their own private world of intimate friendship – what the French would call their *petit jardin secret*. Gerard was a regular visitor to her house and they chatted for hours about a host of things: recipes, travel, films, books, families and who knows what else. They were never short of conversation. No doubt Gerard, as well, was observed through Chaucer's eyes.

# Mentor, Mother, Mischief-maker

## Graeme Hetherington

I have strong, abiding memories of Gwen Harwood because I met her at such a critical period in my life, just when I needed to have my rapids-borne boat turned around, even if I didn't know it at the time. It was 1970 and I was thirty-three, recently returned to the university's Classics Department in my native Tasmania after six disorienting years in England and Greece. An addiction to alcohol and a first marriage breaking up soon after it had begun provided the other key elements of the personal context in which the meeting occurred. Nervous about everything in those days, I was made more so by this prospect and as usual I had resorted to alcohol to take the edge off things.

My anxiety was made more understandable perhaps because Gwen was seventeen years my senior, a mainlander, the author of two books of poetry compared to my two published poems, and much spoken of for her brilliant 1961 poetic acrostic hoaxing *The Bulletin*'s literary editor. Oddly enough, it was that other, even more famed, hoaxer in Australian letters, James McAuley, who brought about the introduction, having fuelled my unfounded, free-floating apprehensiveness by giving me advance notice that he intended doing so at a party to be held at his place to farewell a member of the English Department.

The party was beginning to wind down when Jim made a way for her through the still-crowded room and, after the first bare preliminaries had been exchanged, left us to it. First impressions are important, even establishing the lasting tenor of a relationship, and I remember snapping to and shelving my barely anaesthetised angst to the extent of tolerating an empty glass in order to engage with this most unlikely-looking poet.

For Gwen was heavily camouflaged as just another conventionally well-groomed university staff member's wife in a brown tweed skirt and a lace-trimmed white blouse with the accompanying educated Australian accent and confident middle-class social skills. But there the resemblance ended, because at one and the same time she managed to glitter and sparkle like an early morning sunlit Tasmanian frost or river Derwent, breeze-freshened to banish any trace of grey, dead stillness. And this was achieved without any Edith Sitwell exotica of jewellery and clothing. It came from the inner animation that informed her features, movements and words. Small, sharp white teeth, a glint and flash in the eye, were all part of an impish, mischievous persona that had pulled off the stunning literary coup of 'So long *Bulletin*, fuck all editors', as was the radiance when she talked about poetry. As she almost immediately did, plunging, as soon as it was socially acceptable to do so, into a precisely formulated enthusiasm for the poetry of Wallace Stevens, having discovered I was reading him and intent on giving me a subject we could discuss together.

Local Tasmanian small talk had got nowhere, and after twenty minutes or so of intense conversation, of confirming we shared traditional literary values, interspersed with quotations provided mainly by her, she left on the arm of husband Bill, a reader in the English Department, the basis of a friendship having been established and her phone number given. Nor did she neglect to look back halfway up the drive to their car, signing off with a memorable smile.

I was captivated, and next morning, free of my usual hangover, I phoned her and teed up another meeting in a few days' time. It was as though she had given the murky West Coast of Tasmania caverns of my mind a much-needed airing. And indeed that is how I remember experiencing Gwen Harwood's poetry before I had met her, as pure and cleansing, coming from the pristine upper reaches of the atmosphere, rinsed in and mellifluously toned up by light. I also thought that this overnight chumming-up must be a question of an attraction of opposites, since I saw my own work in its attempts to soar beyond our miserable, limited existences as having wings too often heavy and dripping with the mud of my comparatively sordid

West Coast mining inheritance. This self-perception had a considerable bearing on the nature of what became our regular Friday lunchtime sessions in the kitchen of her Augusta Road, Lenah Valley, home for the next four or so years, until she moved to Oyster Cove and I went to London on sabbatical leave in 1975.

These sessions often extended well into the afternoon and turned out to be of the first importance in my development as both a person and a poet. I was aware at the time that these sustained, concentrated encounters around the kitchen table were an antidote to the gloom and chaos of my own household, where my transplanted English wife was failing to cope with her endogenous depression and the mothering of two infant daughters. Gwen's brimming, bubbling-over quicksilver personality was something I looked forward to, that helped to get me through the teaching week. It seemed calculated to lighten my mood as we exchanged 'shop' or university talk, mulled over each other's recent poems, our work in progress, not to mention our fortunes, good and bad, in what she called 'the jungle of Australian poetry'. All editors were 'red in tooth and claw', critics were embittered would-be creative writers, unless they happened to be both. All this was delivered with a lightness of touch, with an often mercurial, capricious disregard for the strict truth of the matter, which would have restricted the high-spirited sounding-off we both so much enjoyed. I never left her company without feeling refreshed and at least temporarily relieved of the always imminent prospect of a wife labouring to accept living in Tasmania about to be shot into a clinic again for more ECT treatment. And into the bargain I went away flattered, with Gwen ever generous and intent on treating me as her equal, having spoken of my West Coast of Tasmania-based poems as 'well earthed', as having 'salted' her life with another, grimmer reality. It made me think that she'd perhaps been reading too much Wittgenstein and was in need of breathing less rarefied air.

During these working lunches, Gwen and I were essentially confined to the kitchen, with Bill having the run of the rest of the house, although, weather permitting, he'd often be out in the backyard building his yacht, called, I think, *Iris*, if it wasn't *Sappho*. It was one of those feats of skill in the handyman world of Tasmania that my hopelessly impractical self always marvelled at in a slightly resentful, half-embarrassed way. I don't remember him once coming into the kitchen while we were there and I used to hope he'd already eaten. He certainly didn't encourage conversation when I greeted him on arrival, but on occasion I'd have afternoon tea with both of them in the sitting room before proceeding to the New Sydney Hotel, where what passed for a small bohemian element used to hang out in those days. Neither Gwen nor Bill ever accompanied me there to get started on yet another lost weekend. And in all honesty I have to say I rather dreaded the afternoon teas that sometimes concluded my almost weekly visits, since Bill was still basically unforthcoming, and Gwen too could then unhelpfully switch off and add to a silence of nightmarish proportions, broken only by my finding the courage to rise and take my leave for a steadying drink or two.

While I can't say that Bill initially resented my Augusta Road visits in any active way, at the same time he did no more than a polite bare minimum to make me feel welcome. After all, I was his much younger, heavy-drinking colleague who did nothing for his boat-building hobby or his professional work with computers and linguistics, having as a callow, unappreciative student years earlier attended very few of his lectures on semantics and in the exam received the five per cent I deserved. Frostiness and an inclination to repay my attitude in kind were only natural and fair at the beginning. Over a two- or three-year period he did slowly thaw, until finally he could bring himself to come to my room at the university and invite me to contribute my knowledge of ancient epic literature to an honours course he and Thea Goodwin were running on the Anglo-Saxon equivalent, Gwen responding through gritted teeth with 'about bloody time!' With things grown more relaxed, Bill only once thereafter let show a mild, acceptable streak of malice by telling me, when Gwen had a female poet staying, that I was free to join the other lady poets.

Gwen's instinctive womanly flirtatiousness was, I recall, well within bounds when she picked me up late Friday mornings outside the Quayle Street squash centre after my game. Pulling up in the car, she would greet me with a fluttering of eyelids painted with a green mascara, touch my lips with hers, squeeze my hand, address me as 'honey child', and we'd be off to the kitchen to see what we'd cooked up during the week.

There's nothing like a hard game of squash to make you feel relaxed, and it greatly helped me to settle down to being cooped up in the kitchen with Gwen. I don't mean to suggest it was anything in the nature of an ordeal to be thus situated for two or three hours at a stretch, but Gwen was a highly tuned, tightly wound-up sort of person, and tension and anxiety are transferrable items of our make-ups. After she'd given me an art book or a literary magazine to browse, she'd whip around the kitchen preparing an in-advance-of-her-times health lunch of alfalfa, nuts, honey, avocado, cheese, tomato, egg, wholemeal bread, and the rest of it. 'Sinful white bread', as she called it, was taboo, but not a large wedge of fruit cake to finish and fill up with. While everything was interspersed with easy chat, the aforementioned literary exchange being reserved for after lunch, I was nevertheless acutely aware of the precision of her lightning-quick movements around stove, sink, cupboard and table. She seemed never to falter as she opened, took out, shut, washed, cut, banged down and graciously served, spending a bare minimum of time on preparation and assemblage, as though her life depended on it. She was intense, supercharged and brilliantly organised in one and the same breath.

There was, though, something of the frantic and the panic-stricken in all this, and I used to wonder if she was in danger of falling to bits. I also used to speculate if the restlessness and sheer unease she at times exhibited, far from making her want to travel, were paradoxically enough too extreme and threatening to encourage her to stray far from the comparative safety of home. But I finally concluded that here was a very rare person who had won an iron control over her demons, who refused the easy solution of modern mindless travel all over the place, preferring to utilise for the good of her art the energies that drove her rather than frivolously dissipating them, taking it all on the chin, as it were, and not chickening out.

Interestingly enough, there was no alcohol on offer to induce or cultivate an artificial relaxation. And that was perhaps the most important thing she taught me during this period of being casually, almost incidentally mothered and mentored: that one didn't need to tone down and anaesthetise what I can only think to call one's inner hyperactivity. If she could do it, then so perhaps should I be capable of insisting on a constructive, poetry-giving, disciplined toleration of self instead of rushing to the comfortable amputations the bottle afforded.

It's small wonder that I, still contending with a serious drinking problem despite having been twice hospitalised with alcohol-induced pancreatitis, should choose in 1974, on 8 June, Gwen's birthday, to share my last ever bottle of wine with her. I'd been warned in no uncertain terms, by a doctor who'd been appalled by the near-black colour of my tongue brought on by yet another attack of pancreatitis, that I'd die if I continued drinking. This decision to become teetotal at the age of thirty-seven represented a rebirth for me, a new life much more in keeping with Gwen's moderation and dedication in service to her art. I don't remember her once criticising me or lecturing me on my ruinous, marriage-destroying allegiance to the grog. She simply let her own example speak for itself, and when I came on board was the natural, constructively disposed, *Schadenfreude*-free witness to my vow to completely abstain.

A year or so previously, she had forgiven me for arriving incapacitated at a lunch at her home given that I might meet, as a fledgling poet, her house guest and friend Rodney Hall, then the literary editor of *The Weekend Australian*, such was her toleration and generosity of spirit. Nor must I fail here to mention her perceptiveness, since she well understood my low self-esteem as a native white Tasmanian from the Hell's Gates mining area of the West Coast and the consequent convict-cringe tendency to obsequiousness, nervousness and acute anxiety this could engender when faced with meeting people believed to be a so-called 'cut above' one's own station in life, especially mainlanders of 'status' and 'importance'. It was my great good fortune that she persevered with me, and together with my father-figure, James McAuley, was instrumental in helping me gain the confidence to stand on my own two feet, though naturally not being able to forgo an occasional witticism about the severing of umbilical cords and apron strings.

If such a multifaceted person as Gwen may be said to have a defining characteristic, it would have to be generosity. And I very soon learnt that she was keenly alive to its opposite: meanness and the various forms it could take, descending in scale from her often repeated generalisations that 'thin-lipped meanness' and 'grudgingness' were the great Australian defects to specific instances of the national malaise. For example, she was furious about the media's scanty coverage of the death of historian Manning Clark. There seemed to have been no tribute to this 'radical' who she considered had so enriched Australian letters as to deserve at least a state funeral.

Nor was Gwen so well armoured with success and recognition as not to register personal hurt. She sent James McAuley, a rival poet, briefly to Coventry because she perceived a certain meanness of spirit behind his rejection, as editor of *Quadrant*, of one of her poems now agreed as representing her at her very best. 'Barn Owl' or 'David's Harp', I think, was the victim of this manifestation of Australian 'grudgingness'. In all innocence she once said she'd like to hold a party with all the poets she knew present in the same room. When Jim heard of this, his response was to the effect that this was naïve in the extreme as they would tear one another to bits. But to bring this vignette into balance, I must record that he thought Gwen as a poet had, to quote him, 'won her spurs'. Another possibility, of course, is that this suggestion of hers was a case of mischievousness and a desire to provoke, skilfully disguised as generosity of soul. Anyway, for obvious reasons I always prefer, whenever I can, to give these two master hoaxers the benefit of the doubt.

I recall too, from kitchen chat, how deeply wounded she was by the 'mean' behaviour of a Tasmanian poet she considered a friend. He apparently stood her up for a dinner date because there was suddenly a chance for him to meet James McAuley, newly arrived in Tasmania in 1961. 'He sent me a telegram from here in Hobart rather than daring to telephone and cancel on the day. He'd cut his grandmother's throat to get into print,' she vehemently recalled ten years or more after the incident. The university vice-chancellor's wife was also less than generously disposed, she thought, inviting her to staff members' wives' morning teas only when she'd become well known as a poet. This inevitably is as much a reflection of the nature of Hobart society in the 1960s and 1970s as it it to Gwen's hostility to meanness in the form of snobbery. She never forgot the withering encounter she and Bill had with the owner of one of Hobart's rare cafés who curtly refused to serve them a meal on the day of their arrival in 1945 because closing time was five o'clock and they'd walked in at five minutes to.

Gwen's generosity was not only of the usually easier abstract kind. She put her money where her mouth was. Early in the days of my Augusta Road visits, we'd proceed after lunch up the long passageway of the typical Tasmanian weatherboard with rooms either side to the dining room at the front, where she wrote and typed. With her four children essentially off her hands and she and Bill rarely entertaining, it wasn't otherwise in much use. There she would speedily tap out any poems I had ready. She rarely made mistakes, and when she did she typed from the beginning again no matter what or where the error was. She didn't like to pause, correct and continue, to interrupt the flow. The copy had to be perfect, with no sign of a fault made on the way through.

The objective was to compile a manuscript from my work since I didn't take myself seriously enough as a writer to own a typewriter. Overriding my diffidence and my protests that it was bound to be rejected if submitted to a publisher (which it was), she insisted I had a talent and therefore a duty to share it with others, quoting no lesser authority than the biblical injunction not to hide our light under a bushel. For a while this was a bone of contention between us since she had divined that I seriously dreaded it getting around that I wrote poetry, as though it would be confirmation that I deserved my unmanly nickname of Blossom, especially if I went so far as to even try to publish it. My only half-joking assertions that she and James McAuley, with their encouragement of my poetry, were setting me up to be crucified because they were inveterate hoaxers really brought out her fierceness, provoking her to condemn as primitive and barbaric the beer-swilling Aussie ocker's rubbish that poets were poofters. She did her best to keep me off the road to victimhood, saying her eldest son John, also a poet, had recovered from schoolyard teasing that queried his masculinity and that it was about time I did too.

Anyway, not to be dissuaded from kick-starting me into trying to bring out a book of poems, into an acceptance of what I really was, Gwen would continue to type, enjoying, she once said, her role as Martha and thereby playfully striking the crucifixion note again. Since she was far too intelligent to leave our dispute in black and white terms and would concede that while it might be difficult for a man to own to the identity of 'poet' in the rougher reaches of Australian society, it was nevertheless best to find the courage to embrace one's destiny. Alcohol-addicted poets like Edgar Alan Poe, Hart Crane, Dylan Thomas and John Berryman clearly enthralled her. They found their voice despite their weakness and therefore didn't die miserably as suicides for nothing, she would encouragingly say. For Gwen had her dark side too, which went far beyond her neurotic dread of the deep green acanthus leaf that had a facility to spread and engulf the garden and then the house, and even herself dreaming of it, she could rather shrilly announce on sighting it near the gate of their final residence in Pine Street, West Hobart.

This showed itself, I thought, in her involvement in operas like *The Fall of the House of Usher* and *Lenz*. The latter especially I experienced, in part at least, as a sinister study in the mental disintegration and collapse of a poet, reminding me of still another dream Gwen said she had of an elephant trumpeting on a hilltop, which she for an unknown reason associated with madness. But she was never heavily and disturbingly serious for very long to the exclusion of all else, and would suddenly and capriciously break the mood by teasingly circling around me playing a snatch from Mozart's *The Magic Flute* on a tin whistle that lived on the dining room mantelpiece. Seeing her in this vein, I would think of her capering as devilish merriment, Mozartian to the core, and wonder if in the final analysis the world wasn't for her a theatre of the absurd, perilously close to the anarchy of insanity, the cruellest possible joke. Was I some sort of opposite number for her, a kind of ponderous, bearish Beethoven type she baited and taunted a bit but was basically fond of? Obviously something in my demeanour brought her impishness to the surface, and as I write this I feel that she may have been tempted out of impatience with me to tweak my ears in passing for being so deaf to the light-hearted, mockingly ironic strain in her personality.

Gwen herself, as I understood her, had no trouble in being a poet, no problem arising from background and expectations of others to overcome, which years later, in 1989, when I left Tasmania never to see her again, she finally and directly admitted could make it more difficult for me to be comfortably accepting of as identity. Poetry being such an integral part of her life, such a natural outgrowth of her roles as wife, mother, secretary/receptionist, lover of the arts and friend, everything was grist to the mill, and it wasn't long before I appeared in one of her poems as 'a wound-gash opens in the west'. And I was a bit startled to hear that the sharp chop bones on our plates had become in a dream a sword embedded in my head, which found its way into one of her Tristan and Isolde poems. Another, 'Herongate', dedicated to me, came out of an exchange of poems, and I felt flattered to be part of her rich and varied consciousness. Not surprisingly, out of all this there resulted seven poems from me named for her over our twenty-five-year period of contact.

As already implied, Gwen's sensibility was much too developed and refined for her, if she were legally permitted, to be at home in the Hobart bars of the 1970s, though changes for the better were under way by then. She would duck my invitations with the excuse that anything more than a glass of wine with a meal gave her a headache. This, I soon worked out, meant she had too much respect for her brain, which was in line with her fierce dislike of boxing on the grounds that it was idiotic to batter that part of the body housing the mind, the only instrument we have with which to try to ennoble ourselves. I don't mean any of this to suggest she was fanatically disposed or prudish. She certainly wasn't. It was just that she and Bill arrived in Tasmania civilised and with interests other than racehorses, greyhounds, footy, booze, golf and bowls. I remember them as ultra-educated middle-class folk normally and logically appreciative of the material comforts inner-city Hobart suburban life gave, and taken up with pursuits demanding peace and quiet and being alone in a room, with perhaps an exception being made for FM radio turned down low in the background.

Gwen's habits and lifestyle were an obvious clear-cut alternative to the cultural desert inhabited by eternally whingeing Hobartian malcontents, young Education Department teachers, wannabes and disadvantaged Commonwealth Rehabilitation Training Scheme or CRTS blokes who'd tragically missed the boat because of war service, and seemed, many of them, to have nothing better to do than console themselves with alcohol all weekend. But there were hazards to be encountered when suddenly I cold-turkeyed and shifted from one world to the other at thirty-seven, free at last from the life-threatening encumbrance of alcoholism. These could take the shape of loyalties being put to the test as the legacy from my most recent past followed me around the small town.

One of them directly involved Gwen when I discovered that by a strange, complicating coincidence a boon companion I'd been obliged to break away from was her next-door neighbour in Pine Street, West Hobart, the Harwoods having moved back to town in 1985 after ten years at Oyster Cove, near Kettering. I used to feel embarrassed, deeply guilty even, that I was welcome to visit Gwen but he wasn't. I'd spent many a lost weekend in my former life in the company of this much older man who was the quintessence of Hobart's demi-monde with all its hopelessness and despair attendant upon failed aspirations. The CTRS had given him a chance after the war to go to art school and become a painter, but personal inadequacies had proved him unequal to the occasion and he'd fetched up pretty rough, in old age renting a unit overlooking Gwen's backyard. He was, really, an interesting mix of the noble innocence of Dostoyevsky's Prince Myshkin in *The Idiot* and the ratbag bohemianism of Joyce Carey's Gully Jimson in *The Horse's Mouth*. Now well into his terminal decline with an ulcerated leg, he was spending his last days before hospitalisation among piles of unwashed dishes, his unfinished paintings barely visible amidst the clutter and mostly turned in shame to face the walls. The contrast with Gwen and her burgeoning achievement was nothing short of astonishing, and heart-breaking into the bargain. She knew him by sight and reputation garnered via some of the members of his Saturday morning Adult Education painting class who'd had to tolerate his instruction heavily handicapped by appalling hangovers and held on the waterfront, regardless of the weather, close to one of the pubs. But apart from a 'hello' over the back fence and a pleasantry or two exchanged, with him gallantly raising his beret as they passed on their way to or from the local shop, the relationship foundered and stalled on their mutual awareness of their utterly different circumstances.

But at the same time Gwen, and no doubt my life-wrecked friend too, knew there was no getting round the fact that, all-importantly, they shared the creative impulse, that they were fellow artists no matter how different the result had been for each of them. Accordingly, she felt uncomfortable with the situation, if not, for all I know, downright mortified. It was one of those impossible impasses and she never resolved the problem, uncharacteristically hiding behind Bill's worsening health and reclusive tendency to lamely justify not inviting him in, shakes, delirium tremens, rotting limb and all, for a cup of tea and a biscuit. 'You know Bill!' she said to me on more than one occasion. For me, it was not so difficult. I simply went to see him from time to time, but on the sly, and happy not to run into the Harwoods when I did, an indefinable sense of guilt somehow tied to Tasmania's wretched convict past continuing to cast its shadow.

Gwen had a poet's idealism and yearning for the world to be a better place, a longing to fly in the face of our tragic, limited natures, which only great art could transcend and redeem. She had a habit of deeply sighing, her way of saying 'if only –'. A strong sense of transience and of our mortality defined her, I think, as having a more pessimistic than optimistic cast of mind. Politically, she emerged for me as considerably more to the left than the right, though she was by no means passionately committed to any cause or ideology that I knew of. Her four children went to The Friends' School, a private school, because, as I remember her saying, 'at least the Quakers have their hearts in the right place', and anyway that's where she and Bill thought the best education was available. It was also within easy walking distance of their Lenah Valley home. Common sense and a strong connection with the realities were always in evidence with her.

I remember too that she admired the Australian 'battler' type, of which Tasmania has an abundance, and her conversation was dotted with instances of the trials and tribulations of ordinary folk barely making a go of it. It was the greater generosity and inclusiveness of the Labor Party, its more humane face, that distinguished it for her from its Liberal counterpart, though Bill, as an ex-naval serviceman, spoke up heatedly on behalf of the American alliance and special friendship that went with it as obviously being in the best interests of our survival. Feminism as a movement was fast establishing itself when I first knew Gwen, but she certainly didn't have a consuming, besotted regard, or indeed any use, for it. She drove the car, was free to come and go, had a job and was successfully competing with her poetry among men because of its inherent merit. Specially pleading didn't tempt her and was seen as ultimately counter-productive.

From the above, it need be no surprise that she made an emotional response to any perceived injustice. The fair-go, fair-play ethic was uppermost in her nature and she could be fierce in her defence and protection of shabbily treated friends. For example, it still rankled, ten years after the event, that the modest-to-a-fault, academically better and more relevantly qualified Ted Stokes had missed out on the Chair of English at the University of Tasmania because show pony, charismatic James McAuley, the successful applicant, had powerful literary mates like Alec Hope and the professor of English at Melbourne University on the selection committee. This, she thought, was a case where the special consideration of the local university needing a high-profile professor in the wake of the image-damaging Orr fiasco had resulted in a back-room deal being done. Celebrity status had triumphed over solid academic qualifications and achievement. It should never have been permitted to happen, she would protest.

Gwen was also quick to let me know that much as she admired the lyricism of James McAuley's shorter poems, she didn't share his conservative anti-modernism or his right-wing religious and political convictions. She thought his DLP Labor-Party-splitting activities were below the belt and that the sinisterly dark-suited Bob Santamaria, with whom Jim was in cahoots, was a fluent scoundrel in league with the Devil himself. She considered they were both paranoid about the threat of communism in Australia, that it was a case of 'reds under the bed'. And when Jim appointed a Catholic priest to the English Department, she thought it was rampant papistry, and she always drily referred to the man as 'the priest', never by name. But the worst she had against my other 'mentor' and 'father-figure' to boot was she had it on good authority that when he visited Melbourne, he triggered her friend and fellow poet Vincent Buckley's drinking bouts, thereby putting Jim on the same level as Santamaria for Arch Fiend behaviour.

If Gwen may be said to have had an obsession, perhaps it was with the Devil. He came up time and again and she would more than half-seriously suggest that he was permanently resident on the island, as proved by the 'demons' in Van Diemen's Land and the 'mania' in Tasmania. The concept of the 'word made flesh' greatly appealed to her and she would gleefully resort to punning to get the results her moods and conversational needs required. I also recall that she was interested that I, like her, thought highly of Thomas Mann's novel *Doctor Faustus*, in which the Devil of course figures prominently. But more to the point was her remark that a rather vulgar, cheap-looking, check-patterned sports coat James McAuley sometimes wore was reminiscent of the one Mann describes Mephistopheles as sporting during his encounter with the protagonist Adrian Leverkuhn in *Doctor Faustus*. Nevertheless, despite all this, Gwen happily toured Tasmania giving Adult Education-sponsored poetry readings with Jim the Devil, went to parties at his house and to lunches for visiting literary stars in his university room.

If these apparent contradictions could leave me feeling a bit like the proverbial meat in the sandwich and wondering if there was truth in the occasional whisper that Gwen was two-facedly different things to different people, I knew at the same time that this was to misunderstand her. It was rather that she, as a super-complex being, knew only too well that life itself was far from being a simple business, that it was all full of paradox, accident and unhappy coincidence. It was best, I'm sure she thought in the final analysis, to put on a brave face and try to resolve, redeem and bring life to some kind of order in a simplicity-craving poem. I never detected malice aforethought in her or felt she was mischievously disposed towards me. Undoubtedly she had her own agenda – but then don't we all. And when

I once mentioned being the meat in the sandwich, she, with the speed of summer lightning, wittily and tantalisingly converted this to being more a matter of a new young poet coming out between the right pair of sheets! What, I would speculate, did these two devilish hoaxers get up to on their poetry-reading trips around the state?

Though Gwen could discomfit me with her ambivalence towards my adored James McAuley, it was as nothing to the reddening and wriggling of my response when in 1985 she told me that it wasn't only Bill's arthritis and diabetes driving them back to Hobart from their small farm at Oyster Cove. Quite matter-of-factly, without battling an eyelid, she delivered herself of the real reason: the smelly Blacks were moving back and the value of real estate would be lowered. It was best to get out financially intact while they could. Gwen, the pure-minded idealist who could write compassionately about the near-extermination of the Tasmanian Aboriginal people, was at that moment replaced by a grizzling, self-indulgent, materialistic Australian of the worst order. She withered before my eyes into the incarnation of the typically well-fed, overly comfortable Mrs Oz who could feel affordably sorry for the plight of our remaining dispossessed Indigenes, not to mention genuine shame for the past suffering of their race at our hands, but at the same time couldn't face the potential threat of them coming unwashed into her living room.

I realise now that this was perhaps an extreme reaction on my part, even if understandable, coming as it did from one who had worked underground in the mine at Renison Bell on the West Coast of the island with a half-caste Aboriginal man with whom I'd found a rare friendship and experienced as a beautiful person. After all, Gwen was honestly voicing the stock but usually hypocritically silent response of most white Australians when it came to the prospect of socially accommodating those with a so-called materially lower standard of living than theirs, of which a decadently refined toilet culture is such an important adjunct. All said and done, it's perhaps an impossible, unresolvable dilemma. I just didn't like hearing this from someone I'd no doubt unrealistically and unfairly idealised out of all proportion to the capacity of her all-too-human self to realise, let alone sustain. It's the measure of how special Gwen was to me. The fact that she'd 'Europeanised' her Oyster Cove home by naming it with the ancient Greek-derived word Halcyon said everything. Since Gwen and James McAuley between them represented in their poetry the pure high seriousness of the centuries-old European culture I love, they were role models, superior human beings who'd shed the limitations, crudities and vulgarities of young, second-rate Australia. Cast in such a taxing role, they were bound occasionally to let me down.

Reverting solely to Gwen, while I struggled in the first instance to successfully take on board her bluntly realistic, uncharitable remark about the surviving Tasmanian Aboriginal people, I slowly came to terms with it by acknowledging that paradox, contradiction and downright ugliness are part of us all, her included. It was an important lesson to be taught by her, to have to admit that the warts of her persona were inseparably woven into the riches of her poetry, as manure is into a bed of soil producing flowers. Any problem arising from her comment was obviously much more mine than hers.

Writers in general, and poets in particular, are famed, even if their works aren't, for being bitchy and catty about one another. And Gwen wasn't completely above this bad-mouthing. But the few put-downs I remember coming from her were of the indirect and subtle kind. James McAuley, she told me, featured in her beautiful and brilliant poem 'In Plato's Cave'. There Jim is King Solomon, 'master of women, and wisdom of a kind'. He's also Orpheus who'll 'not look back', so arrogantly sure is he that she as Eurydice will follow in his track. The ex-Tasmanian poet who'd stood her up in preference to meeting him never wrote a bad poem, she snapped, the bite of her tone implying that he also never wrote a good one, that his mediocre work lay somewhere in between. Once, returning some of my poems I'd asked her to read, she commented that there was nothing wrong with them, and I was left wondering if she'd found there was nothing really right about them either. I remember too her phoning me to enthusiastically inform me that we each had a poem in a just-out issue of James McAuley's *Quadrant*. And when I said I didn't think mine was one of my best, the silence of her rejoinder seemed to confirm my observation. Was she occasionally the snake in the Garden of Eden she alluded to often enough? I still don't know and continue to give her the benefit of the doubt on the basis of her overall generosity.

It's true that as Gwen became older and more widely known as a poet worth reading she grew more prickly and defensive, more aware that she had a position to protect. When, for example, I asked her if she knew a certain Tasmanian novelist who'd achieved Australia-wide and even international appreciation, her answer was that the novel was a lesser art form because it took too long to say anything of interest. This seemed to suggest no and that she didn't want him straying into her orbit.

The lesser-known composers of modern music she worked with as librettist she thought were on an altogether higher level of endeavour. Or was this simply envy of the greater celebrity status accorded in the popular mind to writers of prose? Knowing her, it was probably six of one and half a dozen of the other. Which is not to question the genuineness of her highbrow tastes. She was undoubtedly an elitist, the champion of her husband Bill and of Ludwig Wittgenstein, both difficult to access, misunderstood and under-acknowledged by an ill-informed majority. Gwen was always strictly logical in her thinking, given its essentially elitist and highbrow basis, though her rare but strong dislike of individuals could perhaps lead to their work not receiving from her the consideration it deserved, as will emerge a little further on.

Compounding all was the fact that the quicksilver, mercurial and even whimsical nature of her personality could make it difficult to know where she stood exactly, if she knew herself. It was a case of shifting sands, for she was a true chameleon if ever there was one.

Neurasthenic and febrile are words that come to mind in trying to capture her. But they seem too extreme. Perhaps touchiness is the better description in my recall of her as prone to feeling personally slighted and, like so many of us, rather too hair-trigger in her judgements. Courtesy and good manners ranked very high with her and resulted, I thought, in the unfair dismissal of a migrant English poet living here as an 'uppity young Pom' and his work not being spoken of. A deficiency in this respect also explains her ruffled feathers on encountering one of the male 'poet-heavies', as she called them. He apparently rudely dominated over a cup of tea at a mainland conference with his compulsive chatter and copped being attributed with a 'big, fat, sweating, pink, incessantly talking face'. Another who'd done time for assault still had a way about him that earned him the epithet 'sticker' from her.

Nor did pushiness and networking or any activity smacking of 'relentless self-promotion', as she styled it, have her approval, though Gwen certainly had her own rather high-powered literary strategies. This sentiment was evident in the nickname Busy Lizzie she gave to a fellow woman poet whose fame so far was more as a television stand-up comic. She had concluded, I think, that here was a case of vulgar media popularity being used to forward a rival's poetry whose merit alone should have been permitted to speak for itself. Here perhaps was a lapse in generosity on Gwen's part, the limelight not being easily shared when hype and the camera as much as just the poetry on its own may have helped to gain it.

So Gwen, at the very least, was a mixed bag of tricks in my experience of her. She could be playfully jealous, as when speaking through gritted teeth in mock anger she told me after having read a poem of mine that I'd 'heard the music'. This was a compliment and a warning in one. Getting to be a better poet might mean I'd cross her path and that wasn't without its dangers to me, she seemed a bit less than half-jokingly to say. I told her not to worry and we both laughed rather as members of the Mafia do in films just prior to falling savagely upon each other. Similarly, when she presented me with a copy of *The Lion's Bride*, which happened to be through the bars of a gate in Hobart suburbia, she accompanied it with 'grr, grr, grr' and a clawing motion with her free hand. 'Watch it, honey child, now that we're in competition' I understood her teasingly to suggest, and again told her not to worry too much about it.

Still, though, I keep coming back to her generosity in my memories of her and I'll let them have the last word. And they abound, as when I went to London on study leave for a year in early 1975 with two daughters and my first marriage ever closer to dissolution. Gwen wrote once a week, her letter usually arriving Saturday morning. It helped get me through the weekend before escape to work on Monday, and in a general way shored me up as my domestic situation was resolved and I returned to Tasmania alone. Visiting her at Oyster Cove soon after, I was struck by her loyalty. Instead of the disapproval I ran into from others, in the interests of making me feel less like a pariah she gave me news of her son John's second divorce and impending third marriage.

After any period of absence, threads were picked up as easily and quickly as though it were only yesterday that we'd last met, our relationship surviving my escalating nomadic tendency even beyond her death in 1995, if continuing to read her work and now recalling her are any criteria. The ritual of her giving me a suitably sized grocer's carton of 'goodies', as she called them, was always resumed on my turning up again. These consisted of her home-made jam and relish, flowers, seasonal vegetables and fruit, eggs from her much-loved chooks – though Hector the rooster was her favourite by far – literary periodicals and books; indeed, whatever she'd finished with and had to spare. Her largesse was more often than not a mix of food and culture, and I enjoyed the one as much as the other, being especially grateful that it was through her that I read Ray Monk's biography of Wittgenstein and Peter Conrad's book on opera. But an expression of warmth or feeling isn't complete without a physical manifestation, and hugs, kisses and handshakes were exchanged all round on arrivals and departures over the years.

Another memorable, and perhaps the most important, aspect of Gwen's generosity for me, already mentioned in passing, was her intentness on treating me as an equal because she sensed, correctly, that I felt inferior to her and Bill. This awareness, directly and rather confrontingly once, took the form of her asking me if I thought they were know-alls. I can't remember my no doubt embarrassed reply, but I certainly viewed them as eggheads, in the very best sense of the term. While there did seem to be very little that they didn't know something about, they never in the slightest offensively paraded as the superior human beings they assuredly were in my opinion. They wore their knowledge lightly and yet continue to be the most intellectually driven folk I've ever met. Accordingly, it was relatively easy for me to accept that Bill could defeat me at chess in less than ten minutes flat.

My feeling of having been culturally and intellectually their poor relation persists to this day, but it came, I must say, solely from my masochistically Tasmanian idea of things, not from them. Unless of course Bill's wiping the floor with me at chess was also a masterly exercise in disguised scorn. But be that as it may, on the surface at least there was no indication from them that they thought me the lesser, with Gwen, sensitive soul that she was, always at pains to remedy my low self-esteem. Indeed, she and I were going to share a book of poetry, it proceeding to the extent that we even had lunch at Hobart's Botanical Gardens with the prospective illustrator and publisher, Max Angus and John Winter respectively. Then, regrettably, the venture collapsed because the latter's life suddenly took a different direction. I cannot imagine that this was Gwen the master hoaxer at work.

Gwen was also instrumental in some of my poems being included in an ABC radio program, and during one of my protracted absences she loyally attended the launch of my first bleak book of poems in Hobart in 1986, sixteen years after my initial meeting with her. And after James McAuley's death in 1976 she put in touch with me two people who were writing books about him. One was Michael Heyward, who was researching for an account of the seemingly evergreen Ern Malley hoax. The second was Cassandra Pybus, on whose behalf Gwen wrote to me in 1994 shortly after I'd gone to live in Czech Republic and not long before her death. She warmly recommended her as a friend, establishing her bona fides and urging me to cooperate. Accordingly, I did, and the result, partly stemming from my perhaps too naively and trustingly entering into a correspondence with the author, was, in my opinion, a highly inaccurate vilification of my hero, mentor and father-figure. I was devastated, and because the book came out about three years after Gwen's demise, I was unable to inquire into her role, if any, in the production of this negative assessment of Jim. Had I been hoaxed by her towards the end of her life was, I admit, one of the many questions I asked in my angry response. I will never know, of course, though I like to think she would have had nothing to do with this piece of villainy. What I do know is that she would have been drawn and fascinated by the book's title, *The Devil and James McAuley*, not only because of her own interest in Lucifer as such but, as already mentioned, by virtue of her associating Jim with the Arch Fiend in the context of Thomas Mann's *Doctor Faustus*. I recall also that when inquiring after him via me she would often refer to him good-humouredly as 'the old devil'.

Another instance of Gwen's bounty misfiring, though in this case only to some extent, concerns the indefinite loan of a sabot dinghy that enabled me to fish for both flathead and poems when I lived at Middleton, not far from her at Oyster Cove. I used to row out into the middle of treacherously choppy D'Entrecasteaux Channel, usually without incident, but on one occasion a rowlock snapped and left me without the means of returning to shore, until I thought of securing the disengaged oar with the belt I was luckily wearing. Slightly less dangerous was floundering around with Bill for flounder. I'd perch in the prow with a torch to sight them while he bent over me to thrust with a spear should need arise. It never did. Gwen, I remember, paced the beach and enjoyed the moonlight, probably getting a poem out if it.

If white, Anglo-Saxon-descended Australians can be rather easy come, easy go in their attitude to friendship as such, Gwen was an exception to the rule. With her, it was a serious business and there was nothing superficial in her regard for me as my unstable, domestically turbulent, knockabout life proceeded apace. It seemed to be in contradistinction to hers, and I finish as I began, by making the observation that the basis of our quarter-century relationship came from the attraction that can spring up between opposites. Anyway, it endured, and when I was packing up to leave Tasmania more or less definitively in 1989 or thereabouts, Gwen was available to ferry me around in her car as need arose, I having sold mine.

Storing some of my books in a large discarded bath in another friend's cellar involved calling on Gwen's services, and as she helped me to do this she darkly but playfully poeticised and mythologised the situation by reminding me that in the Oresteian Trilogy of Aeschylus, Queen Clytemnestra murdered her husband King Agamemnon as he was having a bath on his return from the ten-year Trojan War. This startled me a bit, underground in the gloom as we were, since not long before she had responded, again darkly but playfully, to the news that I was once more leaving Tasmania for good with 'You monster! How could you desert me?' So here was Gwen, by now shadowed with cancer, a poet to her fingertips notwithstanding the practical, mundane nature of the circumstances. It was as though she always had to try to transcend things, elevate them to a higher plane regardless.

Finally, since the seven short poems I wrote for Gwen over the years reminisce about her generosity as much as anything else, it seems appropriate that I conclude with them, especially as my abiding feeling is that over the time of actually knowing her I never gave enough in return, and here is a chance to make up with what she prized most, a poem.

## For Gwen Harwood

1.
Your son's third marriage looming up,
Your mother dead these two months past,
We talked all day of grief and loss,

Good humour gilding all you said,
Turning only once to watch
A dark tormented sea run on.

2.
We stood upon a bridge and shared
The river rushing to the sea,
Unhappy till you turned and threw
Two feathers borne by wind upstream,

Then with a third you stroked my hand,
Reversed the flow of time and gave
As lightly as a cirrus cloud
A poem from your childhood world.

3.
Your breast is overripe and falls
Beneath the surgeon's red-hot blade
While distant sunlight like a scythe
Among the black-branched apple trees

Both coldly kills and warmly mends
With pert green buds and milk-white flowers,
Fills up the window of your room
As urgently a new poem grows.

4.
Now cancer's more than just a word
And I've thrown off my island chains
To go forever and a day,
It's difficult to say goodbye,
But something more than au revoir,

A hug from your protective wings
Is needed when it's not farewell
To poetry and love's concerns:
Your finger moves along the page,
The thigh I rest my book upon.

5.
(A reply to a letter)
You dream you are trying the door
To 'Herongate' lost in the fire,
Your muse-haunted house in the dunes
That sang you the song of the bone.
Your skeletal hand turns the key

Before you wake sad but alive,
'My home irretrievably gone',
Your letter unhappily ends,
Though there for a change you are wrong:
In death you will go to your dreams.

6.
(A reply to a poem)
A skeleton white from the heat,
Again you have dreamt of the fire,
Of opening doors, waking up,

One foot on the threshold, unlike
Enkidu who crossed it and saw
Irkalla's flame-smothering wings

And literally died the next day,
As you at an unknown time
Will actually enter and lose

Your bones in the blaze of pure light
You stared at on walks through the dunes,
Practising for when you'd see God.

7.
(Learning to know one's place)
'Hello Graeme, old love, it's Gwen,
I'm sitting on a cloud too fine
For jealousy to let you see,
But please believe your ears as I

Exhort you not to bow to age,
To keep tramping around in search
Of at least one poem that will be
As sure of fame as all mine are.

There's still life in your Hell's Gates, West
Coast of Tasmania being that's
Done well despite the limits of
Its origins encumbering you,

The baggage you can't shed to fly
As high as I have done, or Jim,
Who sits upon the right-hand side
Of you-know-who and sends his love.'

# Contributors

**John Chilcott** had a long career in the public service. He was Deputy Clerk of the Legislative Council; Principal Private Secretary to a number of Ministers (both Labor and Liberal) in Tasmania and in Canberra, and finally Official Secretary to the Governor of Tasmania. He retired in 2009. He has been an active parishioner at All Saints' Church since 1963.

**Robert Cox** is the author of three volumes of short stories and three non-fiction books, the most recent being *A Compulsion to Kill: The Surprising Story of Australia's Earliest Serial Killers* (Glass House Books), which won the IP Rolling Picks Award for Best Creative Non-Fiction Book of 2014. At present he is writing a biography of Kikatapula, the seminal Tasmanian resistance leader in the Black War of 1824–1832. Details of his work are at http://robertcoxwrites.wordpress.com

**Sarah Day**'s most recent book is *Tempo* (Puncher & Wattmann, 2013). Awards for her work include the Judith Wright Calanthe Queensland Premier's Award, the Judith Wright ACT, the University of Melbourne Wesley Michelle Wright Prize and the Anne Elder Award. She lives in Hobart, where she teaches Year 12 Creative Writing. Her work has been widely anthologised.

**Berenice Eastman** is the author of the biography *Nan Chauncy: A Writer's Life* and is a Life Member of FAW Tasmania. Her husband Wal is the author of *Mansions, Cottages and All Saints: Residences and Churches – The Heritage of Greater Hobart, Tasmania*. He is a life member and a former president of FAW Tasmania and its present patron.

**Stephen Edgar** is the author of ten collections of poetry, the most recent being *Exhibits of the Sun* (Black Pepper, 2014). In 2012 *The Red Sea: New and Selected Poems* (Baskerville) was published in the US. His website is stephenedgar.com.au. He lives in Sydney, though he spent many years in Hobart.

**Alison Hoddinott** was born in Hobart in 1931 and studied at the University of Tasmania and Oxford University. Her publications include *Gwen Harwood: The Real and the Imagined World* (A&R, 1991). She edited *Blessed City* (A&R, 1990), Gwen Harwood's 1943 letters to Tony Riddell, which won the Age Book of the Year award, and *The Present Tense* (ETT, 1995), Harwood's final collection of poetry, which was shortlisted for the Adelaide Festival Award and for the Banjo Award in 1996.

**Graeme Hetherington**, although born in 1937 at Latrobe in north-western Tasmania, spent the first thirteen years of his life on the island's West Coast, attending Rosebery and Zeehan state schools before going to board at Launceston

Church Grammar School for five years. He graduated from the University of Tasmania in 1958 and went to teach in its Classics Department for over twenty-three years before going to live in Europe in 1989. He returned to Tasmania in 2013 and is the author of four books of poetry.

**Giles Hugo,** born in South Africa, is a journalist (retired), photographer and sometime writer. Dozens of his short stories have been published in South Africa, UK, US, Tanzania and Australia. He has produced several book covers and one CD cover, and specialises in shooting (not literally) writers, artists, pool players, spiders, skyscapes, street life and abstract weirdness. He is preparing for his first exhibition (commissions welcomed – end of gratuitous plug). He lives in Hobart with wife, poet and muse Anne Kellas.

**Don Kay** was born in Smithton, Tasmania, in 1933, the youngest of six children. After completing his primary and secondary education in Tasmania, he gained his music degree in Melbourne. He studied composition privately in London with Malcolm Williamson from 1959 to 1964 while also teaching music at Peckham Manor School and raising a young family. Returning to Tasmania as Lecturer in Music at Hobart Teachers' College in 1965, he joined the staff of the Tasmanian Conservatorium of Music as Lecturer in Composition and Music Education in 1967. He has taught and composed throughout his career to this day, with performances, recordings and broadcasts both nationally and internationally. He has had both local and overseas publications of a diverse range of works. His libretti collaborators have included Clive Sansom (two works), Gwen Harwood (four works) and, most recently, John Honey, with three works, culminating in his three-act opera *The Bushranger's Lover* in 2012.

**Robyn Mathison** was born in Narrandera, NSW, in 1938 and has lived in Hobart since 1975. She has been having work published in journals and anthologies for many years. She has also co-edited three anthologies of Tasmanian writing: *Past the Poppies* (FAW Tasmania, 1996) with Megan Schaffner; *Republican Dreaming* (Bumblebee Books, 1999); and *Moorilla Mosaic* (Bumblebee Books, 2001) with Lyn Reeves. Her poetry collection *To Be Eaten By Mice* was published by Ginninderra Press in 2009. She is a life member of the FAW, the Tasmanian Writers Centre and the Society of Women Writers.

**Tim Thorne** (born 1944) lives in Launceston, Tasmania. He is the author of fourteen volumes of poetry, the most recent of which is *The Unspeak Poems and other verses* (Walleah Press, 2014). He won the William Baylebridge Award for *A Letter to Egon Kisch* (2007) and in 2012 the Christopher Brennan Award. He was director of the Tasmanian Poetry Festival from 1985 to 2001 and is a life member of the Tasmanian Writers' Centre.

**Janet Upcher,** who lives in Hobart, has just published a monograph on the writing of Margaret Scott, *Changing Countries, Bridging Worlds* (Ginninderra Press, 2014).

As well as writing, she teaches, and she has taught in just about every sector of Tasmanian education, including TCAE, UTAS, several Hobart colleges, state secondary schools and U3A. She is also an editor and a translator of French to English. She has lived and taught in France and still loves travelling to see friends and colleagues there, although her greatest joy is always visits to and from her two sons.

**Gae Williams**'s teaching career encompassed Campbell St School, Camp Hill, in Brisbane, Middle School in Morden, UK, and Blackmans Bay. She taught at South Hobart School on Fridays for several years. The last decades of her teaching and learning were spent coordinating special programs within her own school and clusters of schools, the intent being to involve all students in creative learning and to involve the community in that learning.

www.ingramcontent.com/pod-product-compliance
Lightning Source LLC
Chambersburg PA
CBHW062147100526
44589CB00014B/1720